Magical CROSS STITCH

OVER 25 ENCHANTING FANTASY DESIGNS

D&C

David and Charles

A DAVID & CHARLES BOOK
Copyright © David & Charles Limited 2006

David & Charles is an F+W Publications Inc. company
4700 East Galbraith Road
Cincinnati, OH 45236

First published in the UK in 2006

Designs copyright © Claire Crompton, Joan Elliott, Ursula Michael,
Joanne Sanderson, Lesley Teare and Carol Thornton 2006

Claire Crompton, Joan Elliott, Ursula Michael, Joanne Sanderson, Lesley Teare and
Carol Thornton have asserted their right to be identified as authors of this work
in accordance with the Copyright, Designs and Patents Act, 1988.

A catalogue record for this book is available from the British Library.
ISBN-13: 978-0-7153-2244-4 hardback
ISBN-10: 0-7153-2244-3 hardback

ISBN-13: 978-0-7153-2457-8 paperback (USA only)
ISBN-10: 0-7153-2457-8 paperback (USA only)

Printed in China by RR Donnelley
for David & Charles
Brunel House   Newton Abbot   Devon

Executive Editor Cheryl Brown
Editor Ame Verso
Art Editor Prudence Rogers
Designer Charly Bailey
Project Editor and chart preparation Lin Clements
Photography Kim Sayer, Ginette Chapman and Karl Adamson
Production Controller Ros Napper

Visit our website at www.davidandcharles.co.uk

David & Charles books are available from all good bookshops; alternatively you can
contact our Orderline on 0870 9908222 or write to us at FREEPOST EX2 110,
D&C Direct,Newton Abbot, TQ12 4ZZ (no stamp required UK only); US customers
call 800-289-0963 and Canadian customers call 800-840-5220.

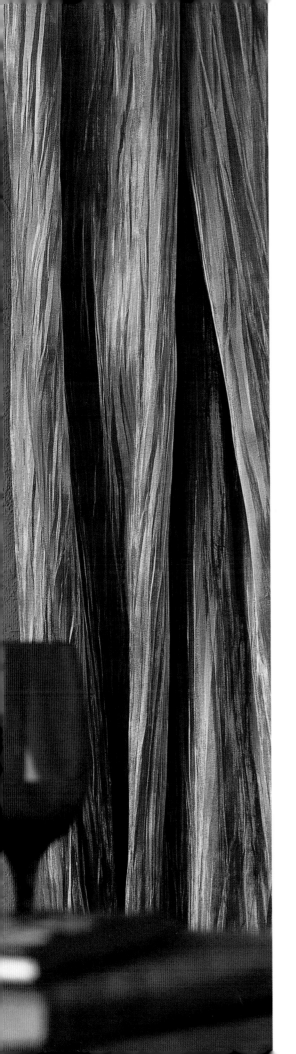

Contents

Introduction

Enter a fantastic world of magic and enchantment and journey through this original collection of fabulous cross stitch designs.

Where will you start your voyage? Astride winged Pegasus flying across the cosmos, or deep in the ocean with beguiling mermaids? Will you nestle among fragrant flowers with the fairies, or brave the thorns surrounding the fairytale castle of Sleeping Beauty? You may instead be drawn, willing or unwilling, into the exotic world of fierce and fabled Chinese dragons. The secret chamber of a master wizard may tempt you to enter, perhaps in the hope of seeing a magnificent phoenix rising from its own ashes.

The choice is yours: this fantasy world has been created for you to explore, and, as you create a little magic of your own in cross stitch, enjoy working with brilliant colours, glittering metallic threads and gleaming beads.

These three glorious designs reflect aspects of the magical world – the power of earth magic, the enchantment of fairy magic and the seduction of dark magic. Stitch the Earth Goddess (page 24), the Fairy Queene (page 60) and the Dark Sorceress (page 40) as individual pictures or all three in matching frames to create a truly mesmerizing trio.

Designed by Carol Thornton

Rainbow Pegasus

A winged horse – what could be more magical? This stunning design shows the mighty winged steed, Pegasus, as bright as the sun in golden-yellow shades, racing through the universe.

The design is filled with symbolic imagery: the rainbow-hued stellar images of the cosmos are a reminder that the father of the gods, Zeus, immortalized Pegasus with a constellation bearing his name. The fluttering butterflies represent the more earthly aspect of Pegasus, belonging to the meadows he grazed upon long ago. The beautifully ornate border, in a lovely shade of blue to signify purity, was inspired by patterns seen in medieval strapwork.

This beautiful winged horse will delight any stitcher; with its rainbow colours it is easy to stitch using just full cross stitches mostly in blocks of colours.

Rainbow Pegasus

This gorgeous winged horse is a companion piece to the fabulous Phoenix design on page 32. It has been worked on white Aida but could be stitched on 28-count evenweave. There are also two smaller designs to stitch (see opposite) – a pretty butterfly card and a scented sachet showing an impressionistic view of the universe.

Stitch count
168 x 168
Design size
30.5 x 30.5cm (12 x 12in)

Materials
50 x 76cm (20 x 30in)
14-count Aida in white
★
Tapestry needle size 24–26
★
DMC stranded cotton (floss)
as listed in chart key
★
Suitable picture frame

1 Prepare for work, referring to page 97 if necessary. Mark the centre of the fabric and the centre of the chart on pages 10–13. Mount your fabric in an embroidery frame if you wish.

2 Start stitching from the centre of the fabric and the chart. Work over one Aida block (or two threads of evenweave), using two strands of stranded cotton (floss) for the cross stitches.

3 Once your embroidery is complete, checked for missed stitches and then frame your work – see the instructions on page 99 for mounting and framing.

Magical Makes

Work the attractive border to create a lovely mirror frame. If stitched on 32-count linen the finished design would be 27cm (10½in) square. Cut a 28cm (11in) square of thick mount board and stretch the finished embroidery over the board, securing it at the back with lacing (see page 99) or strong fabric glue. Glue a mirror tile in the centre of the design to finish.

Stitch count
28 x 28
Design size
5 x 5cm (2 x 2in)

Materials
12.5 x 12.5cm (5 x 5in)
14-count Aida in white
★
Tapestry needle size 24–26
★
DMC stranded cotton (floss)
as listed in chart key

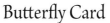

Butterfly Card

1 Start stitching from the centre of the fabric and the chart. Work over one Aida block using two strands of stranded cotton (floss) for cross stitches and one strand for backstitches.

2 Make an aperture card following the instructions on page 99. Trim your embroidery to just slightly larger than the card aperture and mount it into the card (see page 99).

Stitch count
42 x 34
Design size
7.6 x 6.2cm (3 x 2½in)

Materials
12.5 x 12.5cm (5 x 5in)
14-count Aida in white
★
Tapestry needle size 24–26
★
DMC stranded cotton (floss)
as listed in chart key

Solar Sachet

1 Start stitching from the centre of the fabric and the chart. Work over one Aida block using two strands of stranded cotton (floss) for the cross stitches.

2 When the embroidery is complete, make up into a scented sachet, as described on page 100.

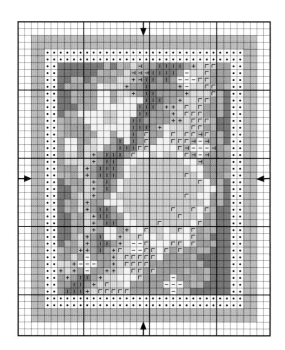

Butterfly Card and Solar Sachet
DMC stranded cotton
Cross stitch

	152		813
	155		826
	451	●	844
┙	452		3023
	676		3042
	727	I	3328
┌	738		3712
−	746		3827
+	760	●	3865

Backstitch ── 844

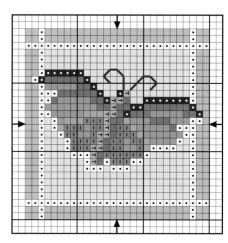

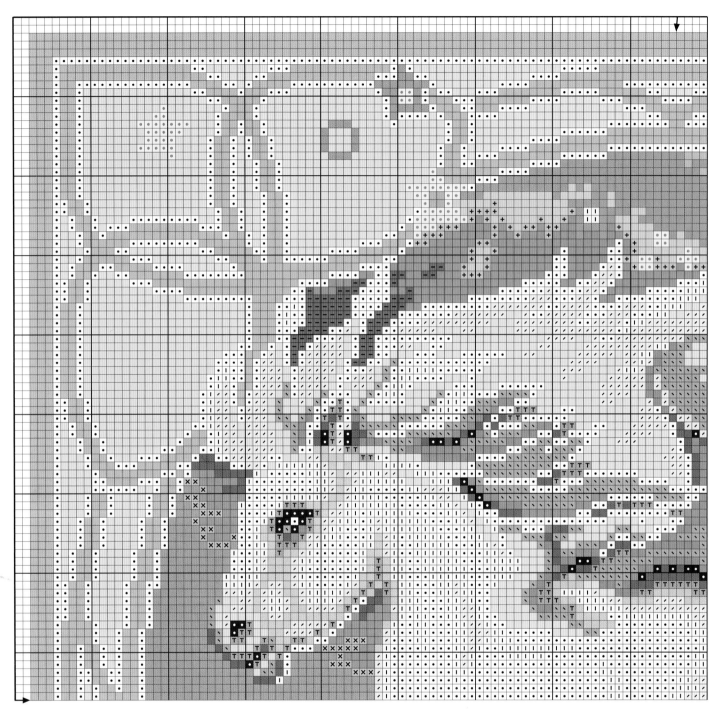

Rainbow Pegasus

DMC stranded cotton
Cross stitch

▦ 152	▦ 453	⌐ 738	◉ 844	▦ 3810	
▦ 155	▦ 676	I 746	▦ 3023	▦ 3827	
✕ 156	╱ 677	+ 760	▦ 3042	▦ 3829	
▦ 451	• 727	▦ 813	▬ 3328	• 3865	
T 452	╲ 729	▦ 826	▦ 3712		

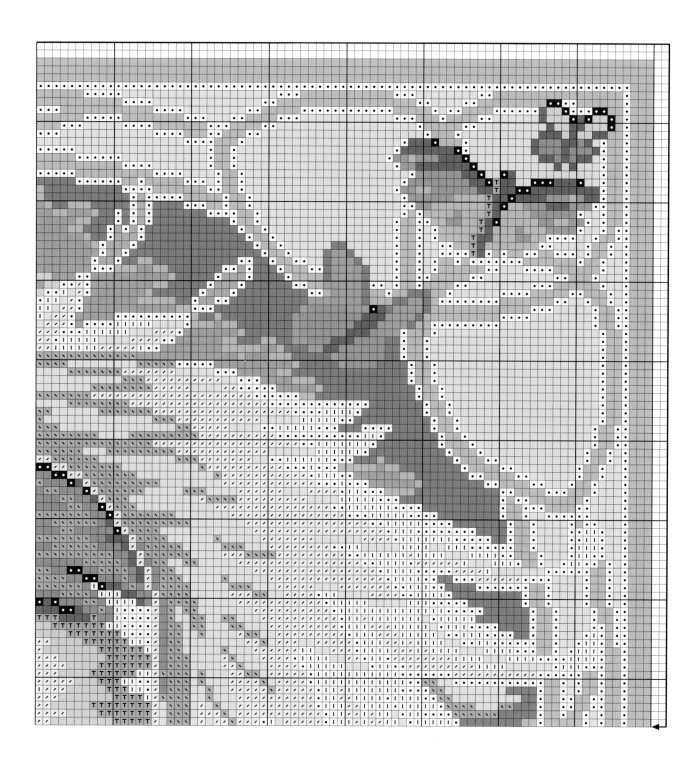

The ancient Greeks told that Pegasus was created by the
union of the sea god Poseidon and Medusa, a beautiful Lybian
princess. The goddess Athena, furious that the seduction took
place in her temple, turned Medusa into a monster, with
snakes for hair, who could turn anyone who looked at her
to stone. Medusa was finally killed by Perseus, with Pegasus
the winged horse springing from her blood.

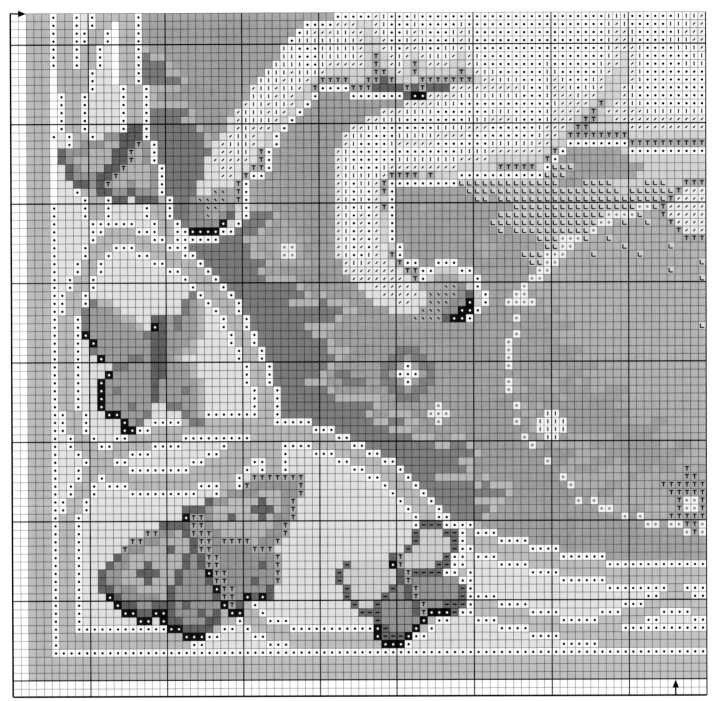

Rainbow Pegasus
DMC stranded cotton
Cross stitch

▦ 152	▦ 453	L 738	◉ 844	▦ 3810	
▦ 155	▦ 676	I 746	▦ 3023	▦ 3827	
✕ 156	╱ 677	+ 760	▦ 3042	▦ 3829	
▦ 451	• 727	▦ 813	▬ 3328	• 3865	
T 452	╲ 729	▦ 826	▦ 3712		

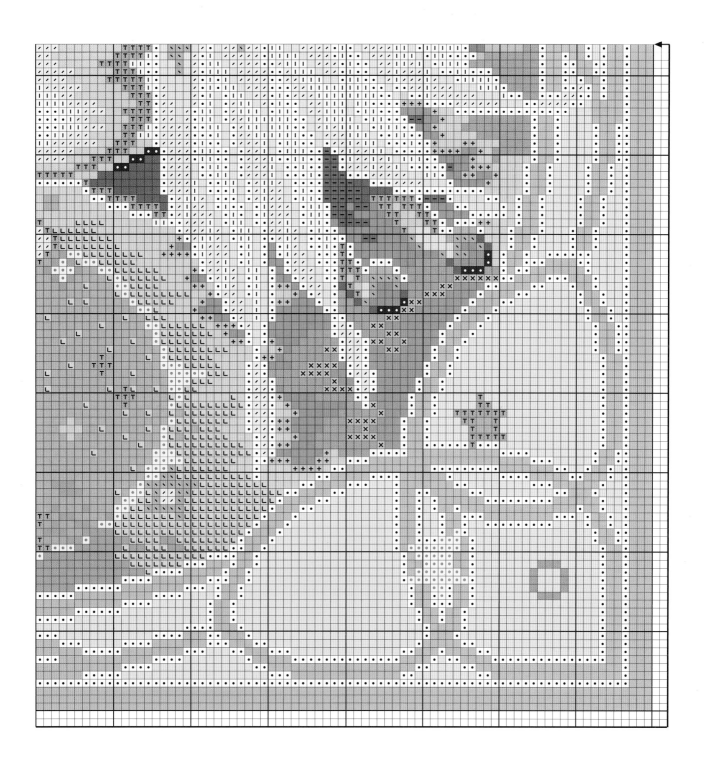

*Pegasus was as wild as any stallion, until the
Greek hero Bellerophon captured him with a
magical bridle. Together they fought and defeated
the chimaera, a fabulous monster with a lion's
head, a goat's body and a dragon's tail.*

Designed by Joan Elliott

Sleeping Beauty

The legend of Sleeping Beauty is well known. Within the walls of her father's castle the beautiful princess pricks her finger on a spinning wheel and falls under the spell of a hundred-year sleep. As the years pass her youthful beauty remains intact and the legend grows ever stronger. The castle walls, long concealed by the thick, thorny branches, are at last discovered by a handsome prince and Sleeping Beauty is awakened by his kiss.

The fairytale is retold in the form of four charming designs on pages 17 and 18, each made up in attractive way – as a journal cover, a drawstring bag, a wall hanging and a card.

The fairytale story of Sleeping Beauty makes a dazzling subject for cross stitch. This design is full of beautiful details, using a lovely range of colours, gold highlights and pretty glass beads.

Sleeping Beauty Picture

This delightful picture captures the last few moments of the spellbound slumber of the princess. Her beauty has not faded despite a century of sleep but her silken dress is entwined with ivy and flowers that have grown through the derelict castle walls.

Stitch count
242w x 186h
Design size
44 x 33.7cm (17¼ x 13¼in)

Materials
58 x 46cm (23 x 18in) 14-count
Aida in antique white

★

Tapestry needle size 24
and a beading needle

★

DMC stranded cotton (floss)
as listed in chart key

★

Kreinik Very Fine Braid #4:
009 emerald (3 spools) and
102 Vatican gold (2 spools)

★

Mill Hill antique glass beads,
03021 royal pearl

★

Mill Hill glass seed beads,
00374 rainbow

1 Prepare for work, referring to page 97 if necessary. Mark the centre of the fabric and circle the centre of the chart with a pen. Mount your fabric in an embroidery frame if you wish.

2 Start stitching from the centre of the fabric and chart on pages 20–23, using two strands of stranded cotton (floss) for full and three-quarter cross stitches. Use one strand to stitch all Kreinik #4 braid cross stitches and backstitches. Work all other backstitches with one strand. Work all French knots using one strand wrapped twice around the needle. Attach beads as indicated on the chart using a beading needle and matching thread (see page 98).

3 Once the embroidery is complete, finish your picture by mounting and framing (see page 99).

Fantasy stories and fairytales such as Sleeping Beauty have become perennial favourites since the Victorian times, thanks to such writers as the Brothers Grimm, Hans Christian Andersen, J. R. R. Tolkein and C. S. Lewis.

The Tale of Sleeping Beauty

Four charming square designs each relate a different part of the classic children's fairytale of the Sleeping Beauty, by the Brothers Grimm. Each one has been made up into a lovely keepsake.

Stitch counts
53w x 53h for jounal
53w x 53h for bag

Design sizes
7.5 x 7.5cm (3 x 3in) for journal
8.4 x 8.4cm (3¼ x 3¼in) for bag

Materials
for journal and bag
20 x 20cm (8 x 8in)
16-count Aida in antique white
for journal

★

20 x 20cm (8 x 8in)
18-count Aida in antique white
for bag

★

Tapestry needle size 24

★

DMC stranded cotton (floss)
as listed in chart key

★

Kreinik Very Fine Braid #4,
102 Vatican gold

Fairytale Castle Journal

1 Prepare for work. Using the chart on page 19, follow the stitching instructions for the Sleeping Beauty picture opposite.

2 Once stitching is complete, make up into a journal cover following the instructions on page 100.

The King's Castle is bedecked in colourful flags to celebrate the birth of his child. As she grows so does her beauty and she becomes known throughout the kingdom as the fairest of princesses…

One day the princess wanders to the uppermost tower of the castle where she sees an old woman spinning. As she reaches out to touch the rattling wheel, she pricks her finger on the spindle and the spell is cast…

Princess Drawstring Bag

1 Prepare for work. Using the chart on page 19, follow the stitching instructions for the Sleeping Beauty picture opposite.

2 Once stitching is complete, make up into a drawstring bag following the instructions on page 100.

Enchantment Wall Hanging

1 Prepare for work. Using the chart opposite, follow the stitching instructions for the Sleeping Beauty picture on page 16.

2 Once stitching is complete, make up as a wall hanging following the instructions on page 101.

This enchantment, cast by a spurned wise woman, sends the princess and entire castle into a deep sleep of a hundred years. As the castle falls to disrepair, the legend of the Sleeping Beauty grows…

Handsome Prince Card

1 Prepare for work. Using the chart opposite, follow the stitching instructions for the Sleeping Beauty picture on page 16.

2 Trim the finished embroidery to within six rows of the border edge. Mount in a double-fold card (see page 99) and tie a ribbon around the left edge as a trim.

Many years later a handsome prince hearing of the beauty sets out to find her. On his white steed he braves the thorn-shrouded castle and with a kiss awakens the Sleeping Beauty from her spell.

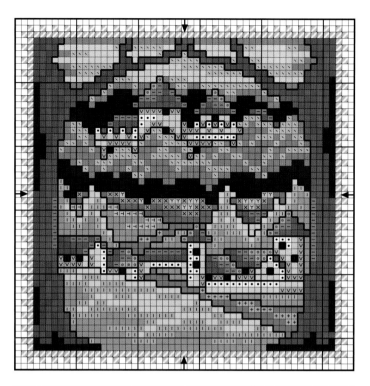

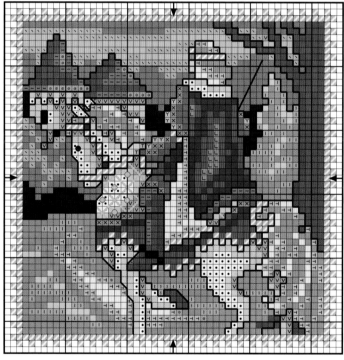

The Tale of Sleeping Beauty
DMC stranded cotton
Cross stitch

156	433	⊣ 729	3325	3803	
V 318	– 434	898	3371	3929	
I 320	◉ 435	T 945	3685	• blanc	
334	501	951	L 3687		
⁄ 341	✕ 502	987	○ 3747	Kreinik #4 Braid	
368	Y 503	3041	+ 3755	102 Vatican gold	
415	676	＼ 3042	3770		

Backstitch

— 3371

Kreinik #4 Braid
102 Vatican gold

French knots

● 3371

○ blanc

◉ Kreinik #4 Braid
102 Vatican gold

156		501	
159	/	502	×
160		503	Y
318	>	676	
320	–	729	T
341		898	/
368		945	
415		951	
433	I	987	
434		3371	
435		3685	
		3687	\
		3688	
		3689	•
		3747	O
		3770	
		3803	
		3929	•
		blanc	
		Kreinik #4	
		Braid 102	
		Vatican	
		gold	

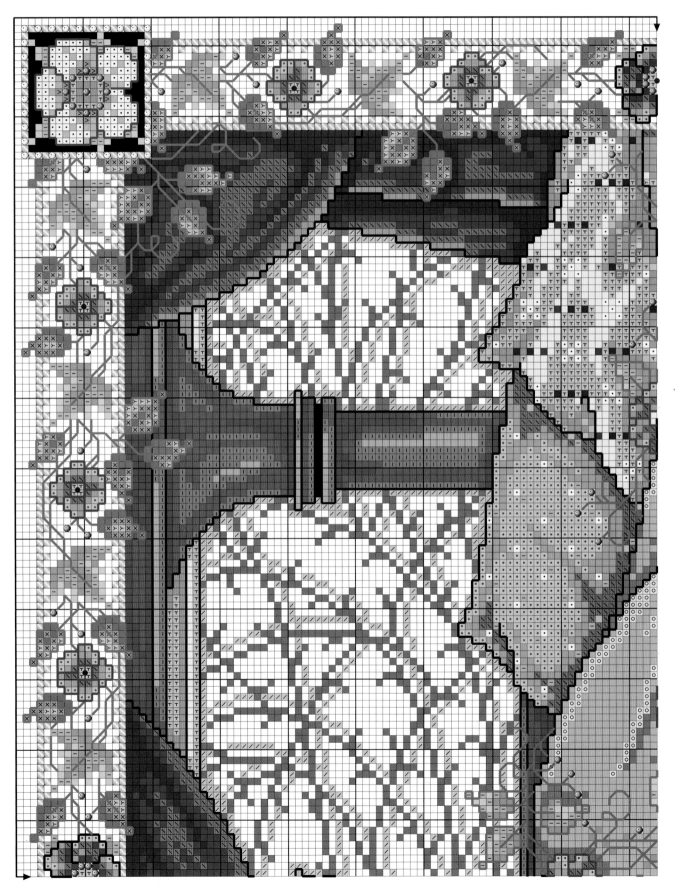

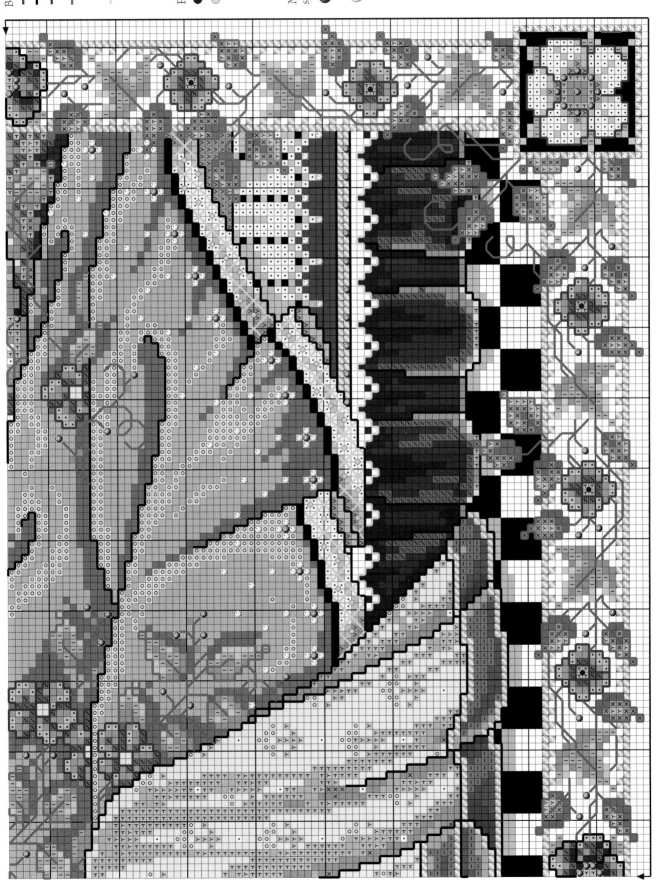

156	159	160	318	320	341	368	415	433	434	435	501	502	503	676	729	898	945	951	987	3371	3685	3687	3688	3689	3747	3770	3803	3929	blanc	Kreinik #4	Braid 102	Vatican	gold

Backstitch
898
3371
3685
Kreinik #4
Braid 009
emerald
Kreinik #4
Braid 102
Vatican
gold

French knots
3371
Kreinik #4
Braid 102
Vatican
gold

Mill Hill
seed beads
00374
rainbow
03021
pearl

Designed by Claire Crompton

The Earth Goddess

Planet Earth in all its glory is the domain of the Earth

Goddess, scattering her bounty over field, wood and flower.

The idea that the Earth is female, nurturing

mankind and all life on the planet can be linked to

many cultures and rituals throughout history. Mother

Earth is also closely associated with the Tree of Life,

a symbolic connection between earth and heaven.

Like the Greek deity, Gaia, this bountiful goddess in her arboreal setting scatters a palette of seasonal colours, plus a sprinkling of metallic threads.

  Worked in shades of verdant green and warm earth

tones, this Earth Goddess emerges from the lush tree canopy that

surrounds her, wearing a spring-green dress garlanded with flowers.

The floral and foliate designs are also charted separately and used to

decorate a pretty coaster and napkin. This design has two companions –

The Fairy Queene (page 60) and The Dark Sorceress (page 40).

The Earth Goddess

This protective goddess celebrates the colours of the turning year – greens for spring, pinks for summer, tawny browns for autumn and frosty blues for winter. The pretty garlands and arabesque greenery have also been used to decorate a napkin and coaster (shown opposite). The designs have been worked on Aida but could also be worked on 28-count evenweave.

Stitch count
237 x 109
Design size
43 x 20cm (17 x 7¾in)

Materials
58.5 x 35.5cm (23 x 14in)
14-count Aida in antique white
★
Tapestry needle size 24–26
★
DMC stranded cotton (floss)
as listed in chart key
★
DMC Light Effects thread E3747
★
Suitable picture frame with aperture
of 25.5 x 48.5cm (10 x 19in)

1 Prepare for work, referring to page 97 if necessary. Mark the centre of the fabric and the centre of the chart on pages 29–31. Mount your fabric in an embroidery frame if you wish.

2 Start stitching from the centre of the chart and fabric, working over one block of Aida (or two threads of evenweave). Use two strands of stranded cotton (floss) for cross stitch and one for backstitch, except green 937 which uses two strands. For tweeded cross stitches, use one strand of each of the colours listed in your needle. Complete all cross stitches before working the backstitches.

3 When all stitching is completed, remove from the embroidery frame. Press gently on the wrong side on a thick towel to prevent the stitches becoming flattened, taking care with beads and metallic threads. You can now frame your work – see the instructions on page 99.

The Romans believed every element in the universe – on land, in the sea or in the air – was part of a single living entity they called Gaia. She was a sacred being, the primordial and divine Great Mother.

Stitch count
45 x 45
Design size
7.2 x 7.2cm (2¾ x 2¾in)

Materials
15 x 15cm (6 x 6in) 32-count linen in antique white
★
Tapestry needle size 24–26
★
DMC stranded cotton (floss) as listed in chart key
★
Plastic coaster with 8.2cm (3¼in) square aperture
★
Lightweight iron-on interfacing

Garland Coaster

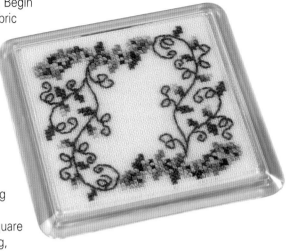

1 Prepare your fabric for work and mark the centre (see page 97). Begin stitching from the centre of the fabric and chart overleaf. Work over two threads of evenweave (or one block of Aida) using two strands of stranded cotton (floss) for cross stitches and backstitches.

2 When stitching is complete, press gently on the wrong side on a thick towel. Back the embroidery with iron-on interfacing and trim it to fit into the coaster. Place into the coaster, adding a square of white paper behind the stitching, and then snap the coaster's plastic backing into place.

Stitch count
89 x 89
Design size
16 x 16cm (6⅜ x 6⅜in)
Finished napkin size
38 x 38cm (15 x 15in)

Materials
19 x 19cm (48 x 48in) 28-count linen in antique white
★
Tapestry needle size 24–26
★
DMC stranded cotton (floss) as listed in chart key

Garland Napkin

1 Prepare the linen for work (see page 97). Measure 10cm (4in) in from each edge at one corner and mark the intersection with a stitch. Begin stitching from the bottom left corner of the chart at this mark, following the chart overleaf.

2 Work over two threads of linen using two strands of stranded cotton (floss) for the cross stitches. Keep the back of the work as neat as possible.

3 When stitching is complete, press gently on the wrong side on a thick towel. Trim the linen to within 7.5cm (3in) of the design on the two edges closest to the stitching, then trim the remaining two edges so that the napkin is 43cm (17in) square. Turn under a small double hem and press. Neaten corners and then sew the hem by machine or hand.

Stitch a lovely border for a garden journal or recipe book by repeating the coaster design on a 7.6cm (3in) wide strip of 14-count Aida band. Attach the band to the book using double-sided tape, turning the ends inside the front cover and concealing with a sheet of card stuck in place.

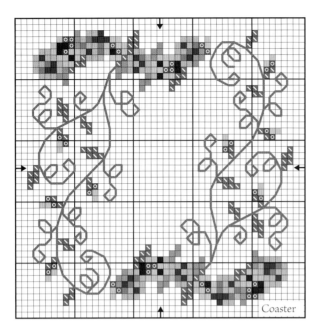

Coaster

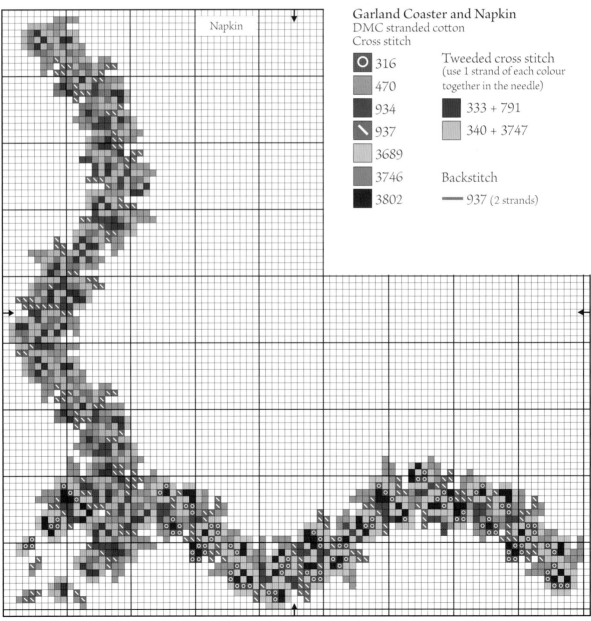

Napkin

Garland Coaster and Napkin
DMC stranded cotton
Cross stitch

⊙	316
▨	470
■	934
╲	937
▨	3689
▨	3746
■	3802

Tweeded cross stitch
(use 1 strand of each colour
together in the needle)

■	333 + 791
▨	340 + 3747

Backstitch

━━ 937 (2 strands)

948		165
3045	−	166
3046		167
3347	+	316
3689		470
3746	/	754
3802		758
3819	\	772
3826	×	934
		937

316 ○ 470 − 754 758 772 934 937 /

Tweeded cross stitch
(1 strand of each colour in needle)

333 + 791	
340 + 3747	
369 + blanc	L
772 + 3348	⊤
833 + 977	
989 + 3348	
340 + E3747 (Light Effects)	
3746 + E3747 (Light Effects)	

Backstitch

— 632 (1 strand)
— 801 (1 strand)
— 937 (2 strands)

The Tree of Life, so elegantly represented in this design,
is an important symbol in many cultures. With its
branches reaching for the heavens and its roots deep in the
earth, it unites the three worlds of heaven, earth and the
underworld and is a reminder of the eternal cycle of life.

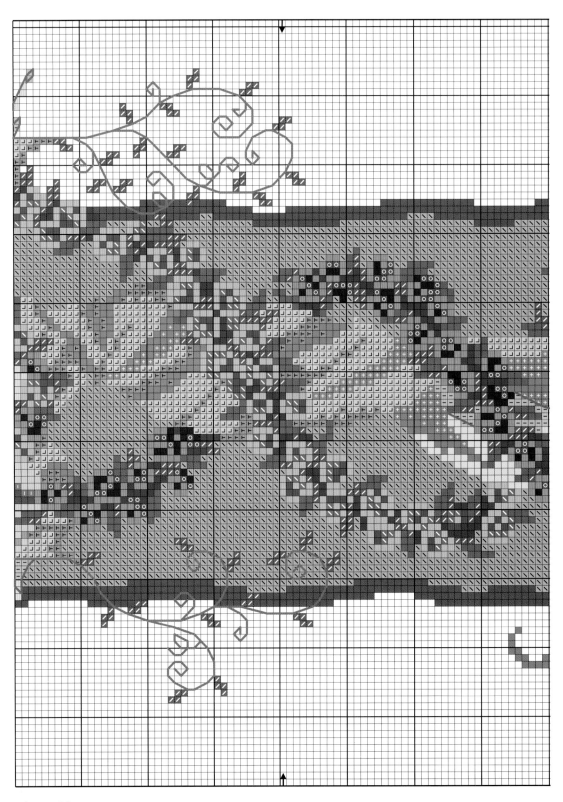

The Earth Goddess
DMC stranded cotton
Cross stitch

948	
165	3045
166	3046
167	3347
316	3689
470	3746
754	3802
758	3819
772	3826
934	
937	

Tweeded cross stitch
(1 strand of each colour in needle)

333 + 791	
340 + 3747	
369 + blanc	
772 + 3348	
833 + 977	
989 + 3348	
340 + E3747 (Light Effects)	
3746 + E3747 (Light Effects)	

Backstitch
— 632 (1 strand)
— 801 (1 strand)
— 937 (2 strands)

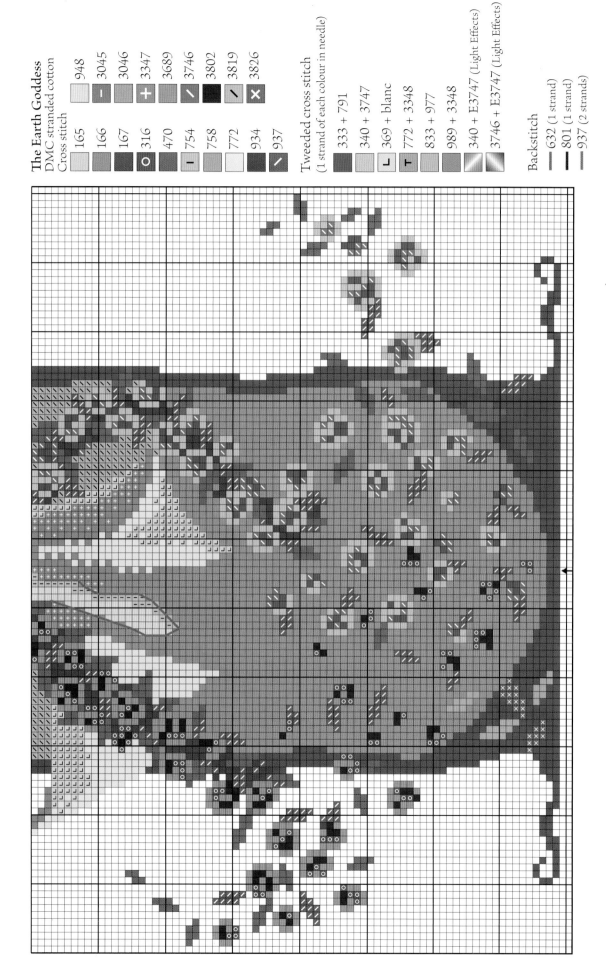

Designed by Carol Thornton

Phoenix Rising

The phoenix is a fabulous mythological bird told of in many legends the world over. At the end of its long life it makes a nest of myrrh, cinnamon and other spices and sets fire to the nest. Miraculously, the bird is then reborn from those ashes.

This sensational design shows the glorious moment of resurrection. The phoenix has long been used as a heraldic symbol and its posture in this design echos that. The solar image emblazoned on its breast reveals its association with the sun. The bird's link with ancient Arabia was the inspiration for the beautiful tile border.

This superb design will be a delight to stitch – just full cross stitches blended in a wealth of gorgeous colours both subtle and vibrant.

Phoenix Rising

This stunning image of the wondrous phoenix being reborn from its own ashes uses just stranded cotton (floss), the clever design needing no fiery metallics to make it glow. It has been displayed as a gorgeous cushion but would make an equally impressive picture or wall hanging (see also the beautiful Pegasus design on page 6). It could also be stitched on 28-count evenweave.

Stitch count
168 x 168

Design size
30.5 x 30.5cm (12 x 12in)

Materials

50 x 76cm (20 x 30in) 14-count Aida in dark beige (DMC 738)

★

Tapestry needle size 24–26

★

DMC stranded cotton (floss) as listed in chart key

★

Black cotton velvet 0.75m (¾yd)

★

Black sewing thread

★

Velcro or hook and loop tape, 2.5cm (1in)

★

Cushion pad 51 x 51cm (20 x 20in)

1 Prepare for work, referring to page 97 if necessary. Mark the centre of the fabric and the centre of the chart on pages 36–39. Mount fabric in an embroidery frame if you wish.

2 Start stitching from the centre of the chart and fabric, working over one Aida block (or two threads of evenweave), using two strands of stranded cotton (floss) for the cross stitches.

Making Up the Cushion

3 Cut a piece of black velvet 61 x 56cm (24 x 22in) for the cushion front. From this piece cut two strips 13 x 56cm (5 x 22in) remembering to have the nap running in the same way i.e. the same way up on the fabric. Cut another two vertical, narrower strips for the sides 34 x 13cm (13½ x 5in).

4 First tack (baste) and then sew the two vertical sides of velvet on to the edges of the design. Then sew the top and bottom strips on to the edges of the stitching, and running horizontally across the tops of the vertical strips. Press lightly from the back.

5 Cut out a piece of velvet 66 x 56cm (26 x 22in) for the cushion back and cut it in half, finishing the edges with overlocking or hemming to prevent fraying. Place together and, folding back 2.5cm (1in) on each on the reverse side, sew back together with the edges overlapping leaving 25.5cm (10in) in the middle unstitched to form an opening for the cushion pad. Stitch on a piece of Velcro as a fastening. Sew together and press from the back.

6 Take the front and back panels and place them right sides together. Trim to size and stitch around the edges, oversewing the edges to prevent fraying. Turn the right way out and place the cushion pad inside to finish.

Magical Makes

This stunning design would make the most beautiful cover for a photograph album. You could also stitch it on finer 18-count Aida to produce a smaller design 24cm (9½in) square and mount it into a jewellery box lid.

In Arabian folklore, the phoenix would appear
every morning at dawn and sing a song so
enchanting that the sun god Apollo would stop to
listen as he drove his fiery chariot across the skies.

Phoenix Rising
DMC stranded cotton
Cross stitch

155	V 351	648	778	833	X 3810	
● 310	535	721	✓ 791	L 834	3835	
◉ 326	– 602	△ 741	797	＼ 3042	3836	
333	T 612	743	807	● 3046	I 3853	
349	646	746	∧ 832	✓ 3047		

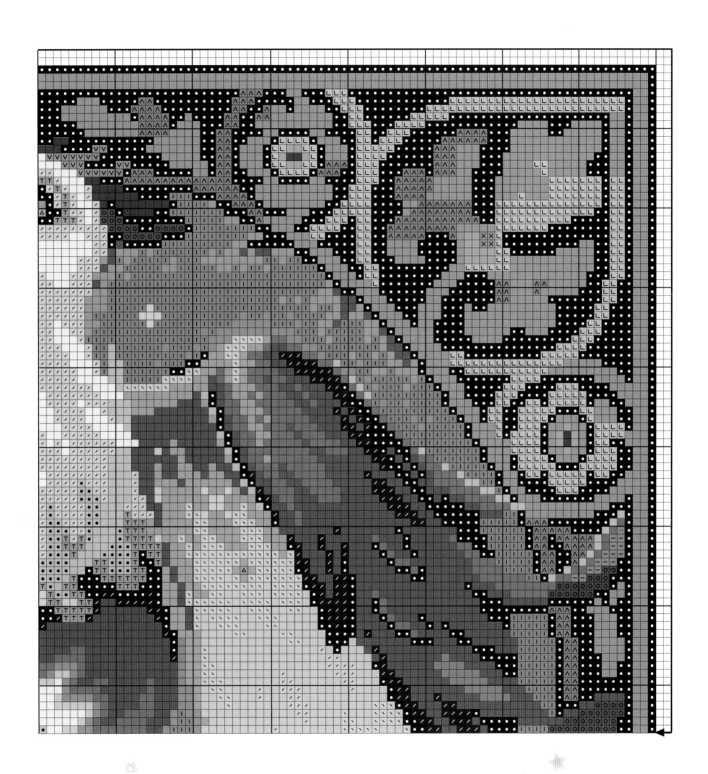

The Arabian phoenix was a magnificent bird as
big as an eagle, with brilliant scarlet and gold
plumage and a song that could enchant listeners.
It was said to have a life span of over 500 years.

Phoenix Rising

DMC stranded cotton
Cross stitch

155	V 351	648	778	833	X 3810
● 310	535	721	/ 791	L 834	3835
◉ 326	– 602	△ 741	797	3042	3836
333	T 612	743	807	● 3046	I 3853
349	646	746	∧ 832	/ 3047	

In Chinese mythology the phoenix was the symbol of
virtue, grace, prosperity and power. Its feathers were
the fundamental colours of white, black, red, green
and yellow. Regarded as a gentle creature, it was
said to harm nothing and eat only dewdrops.

The Dark Sorceress

All dark magic and flame, this powerful sorceress is caught in mid-spell as she conjures her dark magic. In a striking pose, she is draped in a magnificent cloak decorated with celestial motifs, her red hair streaming over her shoulders. She is surrounded by a border of flames that reflects the shadowy forces she is controlling. Magical powers. . . witchcraft. . . is her spell a curse or an enchantment?

This impressive design creates a huge impact by contrasting smouldering indigoes and purples with fiery yellows and golds. Glittering metallic threads highlight the celestial imagery, the cosmic forces the sorceress is calling upon.

In this wonderfully exciting and atmospheric scene dramatic colour combinations are used to create a darker mood. This sorceress has two companions but she is no gentle Earth Goddess (page 24) or seductive Fairy Queene (page 60): she is dominant and dangerous, like the scheming sorceress of Celtic legend, Morgan Le Fay, the fairy half-sister of King Arthur.

The Dark Sorceress

This sorceress is a fantastically atmospheric design and will be exciting to stitch. It could also be worked on linen, over two fabric threads. Further celestial motifs are charted separately on page 44 and used to decorate a handbag mirror and notebook.

Stitch count
236 × 109

Design size
43 × 20cm (17 × 7¾in)

Materials
35.5 × 58.5cm (14 × 23in)
14-count Aida in antique white

★

Tapestry needle size 24–26

★

DMC stranded cotton (floss)
as listed in chart key

★

DMC Light Effects threads
as listed in chart key

★

Mill Hill Crystal Treasure 13015
or similar crystal bead

★

Suitable picture frame
with aperture approx
25.5 × 48.5cm (10 × 19in)

1 Prepare for work, referring to page 97 if necessary. Mark the centre of the fabric and the centre of the chart on pages 45–47. Mount your fabric in an embroidery frame if you wish.

2 Start stitching from the centre of the chart and fabric, working over one block of Aida (or two threads of evenweave) and using two strands of stranded cotton (floss) for cross stitch and long stitch stars and one strand for backstitch. For tweeded cross stitches, use one strand of each of the colours

listed in your needle. Complete all cross stitches before working the backstitches and long stitches. Use matching thread to sew on the crystal treasure in the position shown on the chart.

3 When all stitching is completed, remove from the embroidery frame. Press the embroidery on the wrong side on a thick towel to prevent flattening the stitches, taking care with metallic threads. You can now frame your work – see page 99 for instructions.

The circle is an ancient symbol of unity, wholeness, and the command of the goddess. In this design it is filled with a potent magical symbol of a fiery sun, its power sought by witches and wizards alike. In Chinese mythology, the flame is a symbol of intellectual brilliance.

Stitch count
34 x 34
Design size
6.2 x 6.2cm (2½ x 2½in)

Materials
15 x 15cm (6 x 6in) 14-count
Aida in antique white
★
Tapestry needle size 24–26
★
DMC stranded cotton (floss)
as listed in chart key
★
DMC Light Effects threads
as listed in chart key
★
Handbag mirror with a
6cm (2½in) diameter aperture
(see Suppliers)

Celestial Mirror

1 Prepare your fabric for work and mark the centre (see page 97). Begin stitching from the centre of the fabric and the chart overleaf. Work over one block of Aida (or two threads of evenweave) using two strands of stranded cotton (floss) for cross stitches and the long stitch stars. For the tweeded cross stitches, use one strand each in your needle of the colours listed.

2 When all the stitching is complete, trim the embroidery to fit the mirror backing using the acetate template as a guide. Assemble the mirror according to the manufacturer's instructions.

Stitch count
54 x 54
Design size
10 x 10cm (4 x 4in)

Materials
20 x 20cm (8 x 8in) 14-count
Aida in antique white
★
Tapestry needle size 24–26
★
DMC stranded cotton (floss)
as listed in chart key
★
DMC Light Effects threads
as listed in chart key
★
A5 notebook 21 x 14.5cm
(8¼ x 5¾in) with thin card cover
★
Sheet of acetate
(available from office stationers)
★
Double-sided adhesive tape
★
Craft knife, ruler and pencil

Celestial Notebook

1 Prepare your fabric and follow the stitching instructions for step 1 of the mirror above.

2 When the embroidery is complete, measure the finished stitching for the size of the aperture you need. On the back of the notebook front cover, draw an aperture this size and cut it out carefully using a craft knife. Trim the fabric to within 1.25cm (½in) of the stitching and cut a piece of acetate to the same size – this will protect the stitching.

3 On the wrong side of the cover, stick double-sided tape around the aperture and peel the backing off the tape. Place the piece of acetate on the cover and press firmly to stick it in place. Stick double-sided tape around the aperture on top of the acetate and peel off the backing. Place the aperture over the embroidery, centring the design, and then press down firmly so the fabric is stuck securely to the notebook. On the wrong side of the cover, stick more tape around the edges and peel off the backing tape. Place the first page over the cover and stick into place to cover the back of the stitching.

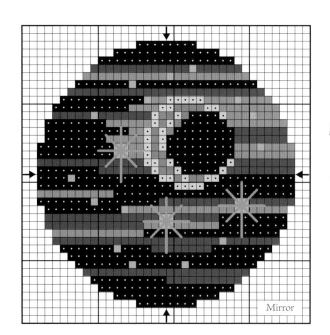

Mirror

Magical Makes

The starry border stitched on Aida or linen band would make a dramatic edging for a bed sheet or towel. If you work on dark blue fabric you would only have to work the gold cross stitches and long stitches.

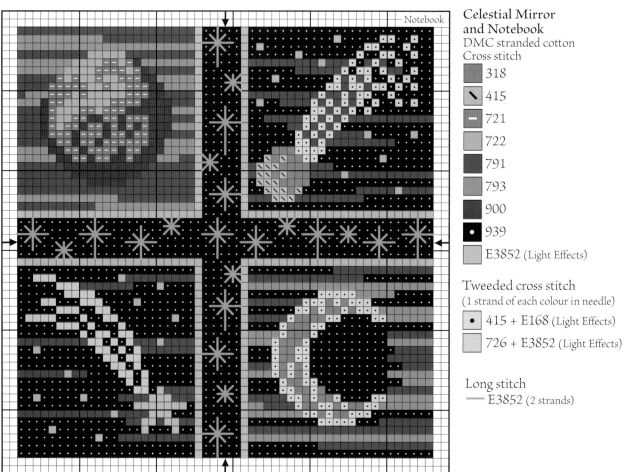

Notebook

Celestial Mirror and Notebook
DMC stranded cotton
Cross stitch

	318
◣	415
—	721
	722
	791
	793
	900
•	939
	E3852 (Light Effects)

Tweeded cross stitch
(1 strand of each colour in needle)

•	415 + E168 (Light Effects)
	726 + E3852 (Light Effects)

Long stitch
— E3852 (2 strands)

The moon has been associated with many goddesses throughout history, such as the Roman goddess, Diana and her Greek counterpart, Artemis. The bow of Artemis is the crescent of the moon and her arrows are shafts of moonbeams.

The Dark Sorceress
DMC stranded cotton
Cross stitch

■	920	┃	154
─	922	⊤	721
•	939		722
	948	╱	726
┃	972	┌	754
╲	3831	＋	758
	3834	•	777
╱	3835		782
	3836		783
	3852	└	791
▷	3857		814
			900

E168 (Light Effects)
E301 (Light Effects)
E3852 (Light Effects)

Tweeded cross stitch
(1 strand of each colour in needle)
○ 792 + 3807
  793 + 794

Backstitch
—— 632 (1 strand)

Long stitch
—— E3852 (2 strands)

Mill Hill Crystal Treasure
◇ 13015

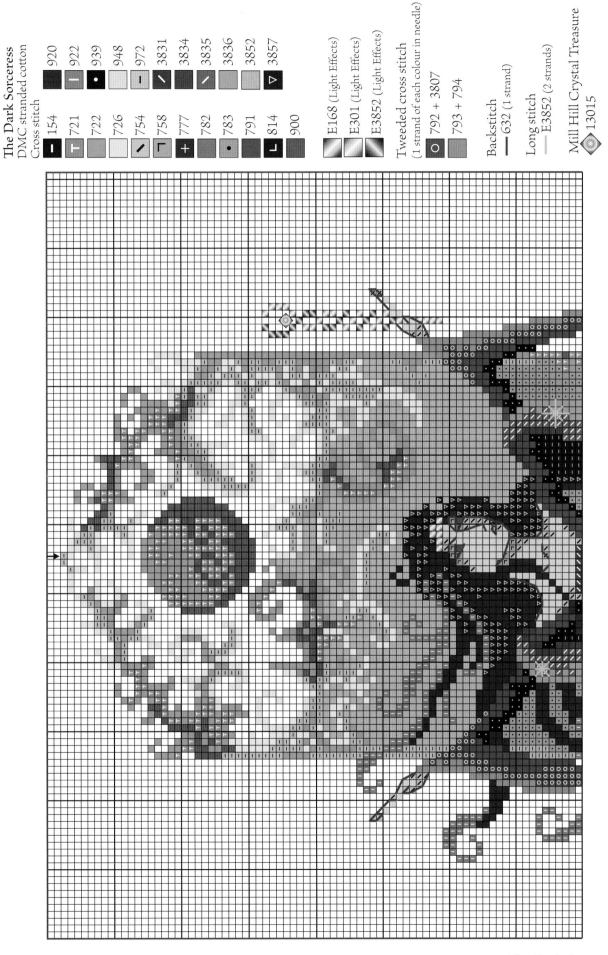

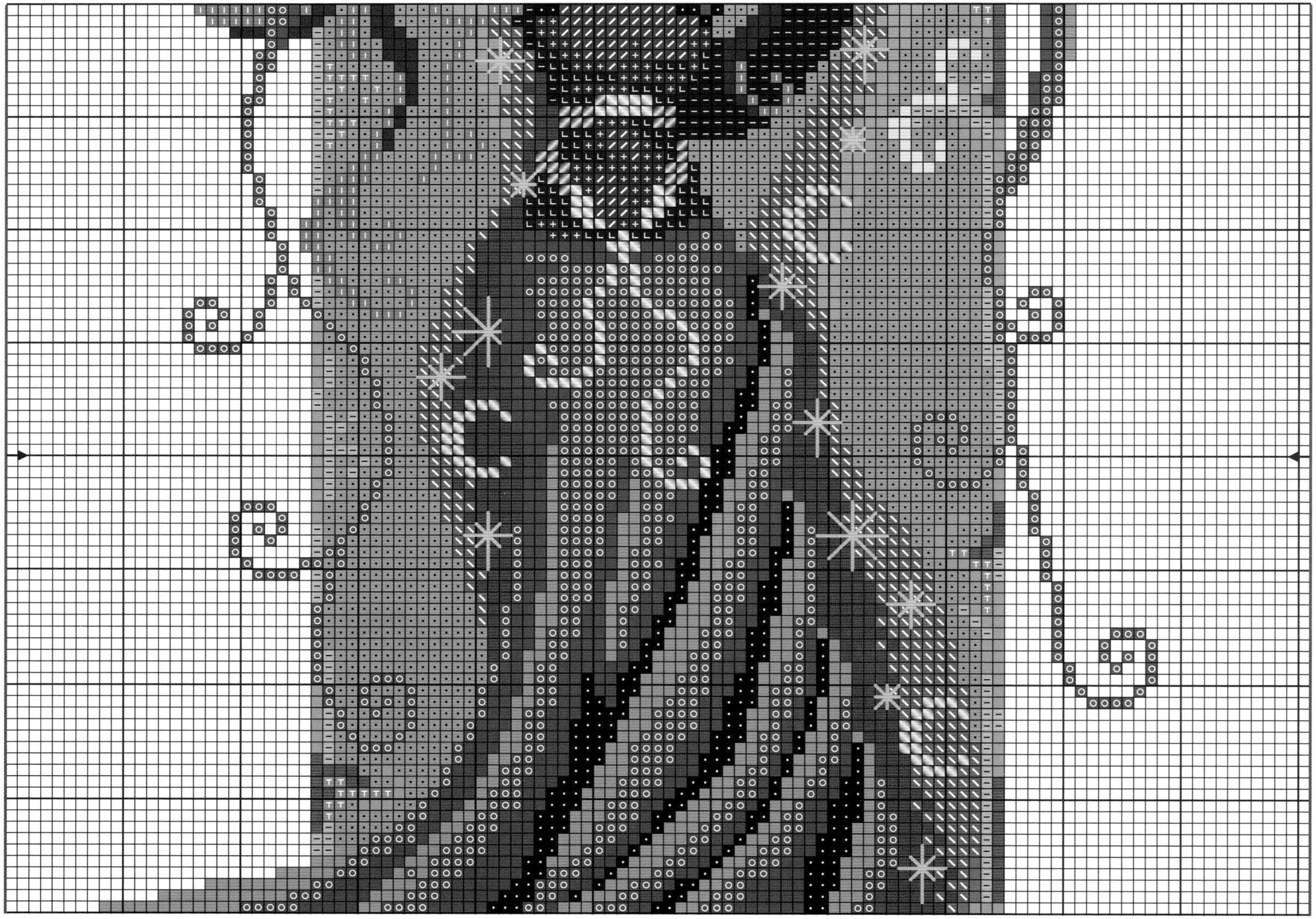

The Dark Sorceress
DMC stranded cotton
Cross stitch

920 922 939 948 972 3831 3834 3835 3836 3852 3857

154 721 722 726 754 758 777 782 783 791 814 900

E168 (Light Effects)
E301 (Light Effects)
E3852 (Light Effects)

Tweeded cross stitch
(1 strand of each colour in needle)
792 + 3807
793 + 794

Backstitch
— 632 (1 strand)

Long stitch
— E3852 (2 strands)

Mill Hill Crystal Treasure
13015

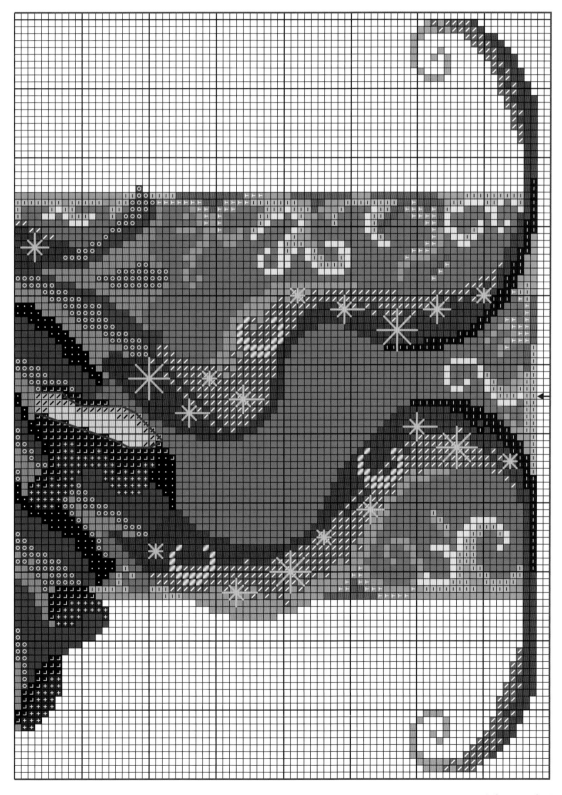

Designed by Joan Elliott

Chinese Dragons

Throughout the Far East, dragons have long been symbols of imperial power and excellence. They have been sculpted, embroidered, painted and written about for centuries, adorning the palaces and earthly goods of emperors and the ruling classes.

There are many types of Chinese dragons and three spectacular examples are shown in this chapter – a dragon of the mountains (right), a dragon of the sea (a picture on page 53) and a dragon of the clouds (a wall hanging on page 55). All are seen as divine symbols of the natural world, carrying blessings of good fortune and prosperity. It is said they can change colour and disappear at will, shrinking to the size of a silkworm or growing to fill the space between earth and sky.

An earthy Chinese mountain dragon features on this sumptuous cushion, reaching for the sacred pearl of wisdom which represents enlightenment and everlasting life.

Dragon of the Mountains

Living in castles deep in the earth, this dragon controls the land and rivers. He soars over the mountains, granting rich soil to grow abundant crops and swift rivers to carry sustenance to all. The bright pearl he reaches for is a symbol of the moon, controlling tides and guiding planting times. His magnificence is embellished with brilliant bronze beads and gold braid highlighting his scales.

Stitch count
80h x 100w
Design size
14.5 x 18cm (5¾ x 7in)

Materials
26.5 x 30.5cm (10½ x 12in)
14-count Aida in ivory

★

Tapestry needle size 24 and
a beading needle

★

DMC stranded cotton (floss)
as listed in chart key

★

Kreinik Very Fine (#4) Braid,
202HL Aztec gold

★

Mill Hill Magnifica™ glass beads,
10080 brilliant bronze

★

Background fabric 0.5m (½yd)

★

Lightweight iron-on interfacing or thin
wadding (batting) 0.25m (¼yd)

★

Fusible web 0.5m (½yd)

★

Decorative trim to tone with
embroidery 1m (1yd)

★

Decorative braid to tone with
embroidery 1.2m (1¼yd)

★

One decorative button

★

Permanent fabric glue

★

Polyester stuffing

1 Prepare for work, referring to page 97 if necessary. Mark the centre of the fabric and the centre of the chart on page 56. Mount fabric in an embroidery frame if you wish.

2 Start stitching from the centre of the chart and fabric, using two strands of stranded cotton (floss) for full and three-quarter cross stitches. Use one strand to stitch all Kreinik braid cross stitches, three-quarter and backstitches. Work all other backstitches with one strand. Using a beading needle and matching thread, attach the beads (see page 98) according to the chart.

The emperors of China believed they were the sons of dragons. Their thrones came to be called the dragon seat and their ceremonial clothing, dragon robes.

Magical Makes

All three dragon designs in this chapter are the same size and therefore each could be made up as cushions, pictures or hangings. You could stitch all three as pictures and group them together or work all three designs vertically on one larger wall hanging.

The Celestial dragons of China were supporters and protectors of the heavens, shielding the mansions of the gods from decay. To denote their imperial status, these dragons had five claws on each foot, while other dragons only had three or four.

Making Up the Cushion

3 Once all the stitching is complete, check for missed stitches and then make up the cushion as follows: place two 26.6 x 30.5cm (10½ x 12in) pieces of background fabric right sides facing and sew a 1.25cm (½in) seam all around leaving a generous opening at the bottom for turning. Turn right side out and press. Sew up the bottom opening leaving a 2.5cm (1in) gap at centre bottom.

4 Trim the finished embroidery to within six rows of the border edge. Cut lightweight interfacing to the same size and fuse it to the wrong side of the embroidery following the manufacturer's instructions. Cut fusible web the same size and place on the wrong side of the embroidery, making sure the edges do not overlap the trimmed embroidery. Centre the work on the prepared background. Press to fuse the embroidery and background fabric together.

5 Glue or sew the decorative braid around the outer edge of the embroidery beginning and ending at centre bottom. Attach a decorative button where the braid ends meet.

6 Stuff the cushion with polyester filling. Sew or use fabric glue to attach the decorative braid around the entire cushion edge starting and ending at centre bottom. Tuck the ends into the gap to finish and slipstitch closed.

Dragon of the Sea

From its dwelling place deep in the waters of the ocean, the dragon of the sea rules the spiritual realm. This dragon is the weather maker; coiling through the sky he brings rain and wind for the benefit of mankind. Worked in rich sea greens and heavenly blues this dragon works his magic above the cresting waves.

Stitch count
80h x 100w

Design size
14.5 x 18cm (5¾ x 7in)

Materials
26.5 x 30.5cm (10½ x 12in) 14-count Aida in white

★

Tapestry needle size 24 and a beading needle

★

DMC stranded cotton (floss) as listed in chart key

★

Kreinik Very Fine (#4) Braid, 102 Vatican gold

★

Mill Hill Magnifica™ glass beads: 10028 silver and 10030 ice green

1 Prepare for work, referring to page 97 if necessary. Mark the centre of the fabric and the centre of the chart on page 57. Mount your fabric in an embroidery frame if you wish.

2 Start stitching from the centre of the chart and fabric, using two strands of stranded cotton (floss) for full and three-quarter cross stitches. Use one strand to stitch all Kreinik braid cross stitches, three-quarter stitches, and backstitches. Work all other backstitches with one strand. Using a beading needle and matching thread, attach the beads (see page 98) according to the chart.

3 When the embroidery is complete, check for missed stitches and then remove from the embroidery frame. Make up as a framed picture (for advice on mounting and framing see page 99).

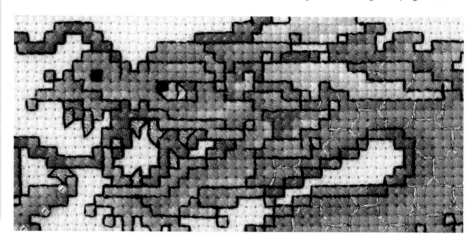

Magical Makes

For something really unusual, and adventurous, why not make a stunning shawl by stitching just the dragon in the centre of a 76 x 60cm (30 x 24in) piece of 22-count linen? Alternatively, you could work the dragon at each end of a 23cm (9in) wide strip of 28-count linen to make a great scarf.

Stitched on white Aida, this beautiful dragon picture is all watery aquas, jades and blues. Gold thread defines the pattern of the scales, while silver and ice green beads convey the glitter of water.

Dragon of the Clouds

Against a dark night sky, amongst clouds said to be the mystical beast's exhaled breath, the celestial dragon supports and protects the heavenly dwellings of the gods. The imperial golds and reds of this divine dragon represent its power to grant happiness and riches. Used as an emblem on the most ceremonious occasions, this creature can ward off evil spirits and grant safety to all people.

Stitch count
80h x 100w

Design size
14.5 x 18cm (5¾ x 7in)

Materials

26.5 x 30.5cm (10½ x 12in)
14-count Aida in black

★

Tapestry needle size 24
and a beading needle

★

DMC stranded cotton (floss)
as listed in chart key

★

Kreinik Very Fine (#4) Braid:
028 citron and 003 red

★

Mill Hill Magnifica™ glass beads:
10010 royal pearl and
10076 gold

★

Background fabric 0.5m (½yd)

★

Lightweight iron-on interfacing or
thin wadding (batting) 0.25m (¼yd)

★

Fusible web and fusible fleece
0.5m (½yd) each

★

Decorative braid 1m (1yd) and
three matching tassels

★

Three decorative buttons

★

Wooden dowel 6mm (¼in) diameter
x 23cm (9in) long

★

Permanent fabric glue

1 Prepare for work, referring to page 97. Mark the centre of the fabric and the centre of the chart on page 58. Mount fabric in an embroidery frame if you wish.

2 To stitch the design, follow step 2 of the Dragon of the Sea, page 52.

Making Up the Hanging

3 Make up the wall hanging as follows: cut two (12 x 10½in) pieces of background fabric plus two 15.2 x 7.6cm (6 x 3in) pieces for hanging tabs.

4 Cut fusible fleece 26.6 x 30.5cm (12 x 10½in) and fuse to the wrong side of one of the background fabric pieces according to manufacturer's instructions. To make the hanging tabs, fold each tab piece in half lengthwise, right sides together. Sew a 1.25cm (½in) seam down the length and across one short end. Trim the seam, turn right side out and press. Now pin the tabs to the top right side of the prepared background fabric raw edges matching and 4.5cm (1¾in) from either edge. Place the second piece of background fabric on top, right sides facing and stitch a 1.25cm (½in) seam all around leaving a gap at the bottom for turning. Turn right side out, press and slipstitch the gap.

5 Trim the embroidery to within six rows of the border edge. Cut lightweight interfacing to the same size and fuse it to the wrong side of the embroidery. Cut fusible web the same size and place it on the wrong side of the embroidery, making sure the edges do not overlap the embroidery. Centre your work on the prepared background and then press to fuse the embroidery and background fabric together.

6 Carefully glue the decorative braid around the outer edge of the embroidery, starting and ending at centre bottom, attaching a button where the ends meet and sewing on a tassel. Bring the loose ends of the tabs to the front and sew on a decorative button at each end. Paint the dowel to complement the embroidery and when dry, insert it through the tabs, ready for hanging. Attach two tassels to the dowel ends.

On the last day of the Chinese New Year season, on the 'Day of the Lanterns', the Chinese people celebrate the good fortune and ideals that dragons have dispensed throughout the year.

This gold and red dragon appears even more vibrant stitched on black and made up into a wall hanging. Embellished with gold and pearl beads and highlighted with gold braid, it would bring drama to any room.

Dragon of the Mountains

DMC stranded cotton

Cross stitch

310	976		
318	987		
368	988		
415	3011		
746	3012		
762	3013		
831	3821		
833	3822		
834	3826		
930	3852		
931	blanc		
932	Kreinik 202HL		
975	Aztec gold		

Backstitch
— 310
| 931
Kreinik Very Fine (#4) Braid 202HL Aztec gold

French knots
● 310
○ blanc

Mill Hill Magnifica beads
◉ 10080 bronze

Dragon of the Sea

DMC stranded cotton
Cross stitch

V	166		993
	208		3755
I	209	/	3810
	211		3814
T	310		3821
	334		3822
•	580		3829
/	581		3841
	597	O	3852
	598	•	blanc
I	746		Kreinik 102 Vatican gold
	992		

Backstitch

— 310
Kreinik Very Fine
(#4) Braid 102
Vatican gold

Mill Hill Magnifica beads

● 10028 silver
● 10030 ice green

Dragon of the Clouds

DMC stranded cotton
Cross stitch

■ 310		351		732	✕ 782	✚ 3023	∨ 3822		Kreinik
╱ 321	L	720	+ 733	I 783	3024		3841		028 citron
334	O	721	734	927		3841			
349	T	722	780	— 928	3821	• blanc	3852		

Additional legend:
- 351
- 720
- 721
- 722
- 732
- 733
- 734
- 780
- 782
- 783
- 927
- 928
- 3023
- 3024
- 3755
- 3821
- 3822
- 3841
- 3852

Backstitch
— 310
— 334
— Kreinik Very Fine
(#4) Braid 003 red

Mill Hill Magnifica beads
⊙ 10010 royal pearl
⊙ 10076 gold

Unlike Western dragons, which are usually
portrayed as vicious, greedy and evil,
Eastern dragons are regarded as the angels of the
Orient, most being friendly, wise and beautiful.

Designed by Claire Crompton

The Fairy Queene

Just as the earthly world has its rulers, so does the magical realm. The Fairy Queene is a powerful figure throughout mythology and has many names: in the Celtic tradition she was Queen Mab or Maeve, a warrior queen. Maeve means mead, a rich red wine that she offered to kings and rulers to signal her approval of them. She has appeared in fiction throughout the centuries, often as a less dark and dangerous character, notably in Edmund Spenser's (1552–99) epic poem *The Faerie Queene* and as Shakespeare's mischievous Titania in *A Midsummer Night's Dream*.

In this glorious cross stitch picture she is represented as a sensual fairy set against a night sky filled with the light of a full moon and twinkling with stars. She emerges dramatically from an intricate Celtic knot framework, perhaps to bring dreams to us sleeping mortals.

Silver metallic threads and beads add texture and glitter to this stunning image of the beautiful fairy queene. The Celtic theme is continued on page 63, with knotwork designs decorating a greetings card and useful trinket pot.

The Fairy Queene

This dramatic picture of the fairy queene is all dark blues, violets and purples, in contrast with her silver wings and the gleaming beads on her dress and crown. The Celtic knotwork designs are echoed on a card and trinket pot, opposite. The designs could also be worked on 28-count evenweave.

Stitch count
236 x 109

Design size
43 x 20cm (17 x 7¾in)

Materials
35.5 x 58.5cm (14 x 23in)
14-count Aida in antique white

★

Tapestry needle size 24–26

★

DMC stranded cotton (floss)
as listed in chart key

★

DMC Light Effects thread
in E5272

★

Mill Hill beads: frosted glass
62024 pale mauve and antique
glass 03044 silvery white

★

Picture frame with aperture
of 25.5 x 48.5cm (10 x 19in)

1 Prepare for work, referring to page 97 if necessary. Mark the centre of the fabric and the centre of the chart on pages 65–67. Mount your fabric in an embroidery frame if you wish.

2 Start stitching from the centre of the chart and fabric, working over one block of Aida (or two threads of evenweave) and using two strands of stranded cotton (floss) for cross stitch and one for backstitch and the long stitch stars. For tweeded cross stitch and backstitch, use one strand of each of the colours listed in your needle. Complete all cross stitches before working any backstitches and beading. When adding the beads, mix the two types together and stitch on in a random mixture, using two strands of DMC 3743 and half cross stitch (see page 98).

3 When all stitching is completed, remove from the embroidery frame. Press gently on the wrong side on to a thick towel to prevent the stitches becoming flattened, taking care with beads and metallic threads. You can now frame your work – see page 99 for guidance.

1 Prepare your fabric for work and mark the centre (see page 97). Begin stitching from the centre of the fabric and the chart below. Work over one block of Aida (or two threads of evenweave) using two strands of stranded cotton (floss) for cross stitch. For the tweeded cross stitches, use one strand of each of the colours listed in your needle.

2 When stitching is complete, press gently on the wrong side on to a thick towel and mount into the trinket pot lid according to the manufacturer's instructions, using a circle of wadding (batting) instead of the sponge supplied, for a more padded finish.

The name Mab may come from the Welsh word maban, *meaning a baby, and thus why Mab is sometimes called 'the fairies' midwife,' as she delivers dreams from mankind.*

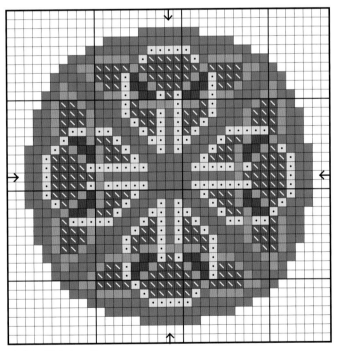

Celtic Trinket Pot

DMC stranded cotton

Cross stitch

■	791
◿	792
■	793

Tweeded cross stitch
(use 1 strand of each colour together in the needle)

■	3743 + E5272 (Light Effects)
·	3865 + E5272 (Light Effects)

Stitch count
37 x 37
Design size
6.8 x 6.8cm (2⅝ x 2⅝in)

Materials
15 x 15cm (6 x 6in) 14-count
Aida in antique white

★

Tapestry needle size 24–26

★

DMC stranded cotton (floss)
as listed in chart key

★

Dark blue double-fold card blank
with 8 x 8cm (3¼ x 3¼in) aperture

★

Double-sided adhesive tape

Celtic Card

1 Prepare your fabric for work and mark the centre (see page 97). Begin stitching from the centre of the fabric and chart below. Work over one block of Aida (or two threads of evenweave) using two strands of stranded cotton (floss) for all cross stitches.

2 When stitching is complete, press on the wrong side on a thick towel. Mount in the card (or make your own), following the instructions on page 99.

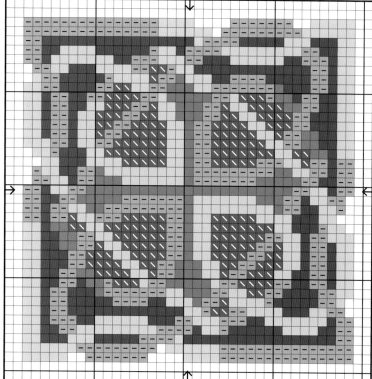

Celtic Card
DMC stranded cotton
Cross stitch

▦ 318	▢ 762	◪ 792
▬ 415	▨ 791	▨ 793

Magical Makes

These small designs are perfect for adorning many objects, such as coasters, pincushions and small scented sachets. As the colours used are limited you could easily change them completely, perhaps to reds and golds as shown here.

The Fairy Queene
DMC stranded cotton
Cross stitch

O	823		159
—	926		160
	927		161
T	928	●	310
	948		318
/	3031	←	415
	3041		754
—	3042	/	758
	3371		762
	3743		791
	3768	+	792

Tweeded cross stitch
(1 strand of each colour in needle)

L	414 + 792
/	415 + E5272 (Light Effects)
∧	791 + 792
—	792 + 793
/	823 + 791
•	3740 + 154
	3865 + E5272 (Light Effects)

Backstitch

——	154 (2 strands)
|||	632 (1 strand)
——	3865 + 5272
	(tweeded long stitch stars)

Mill Hill beads (mixture)
● 62024 pale mauve
☒ 3044 silvery white

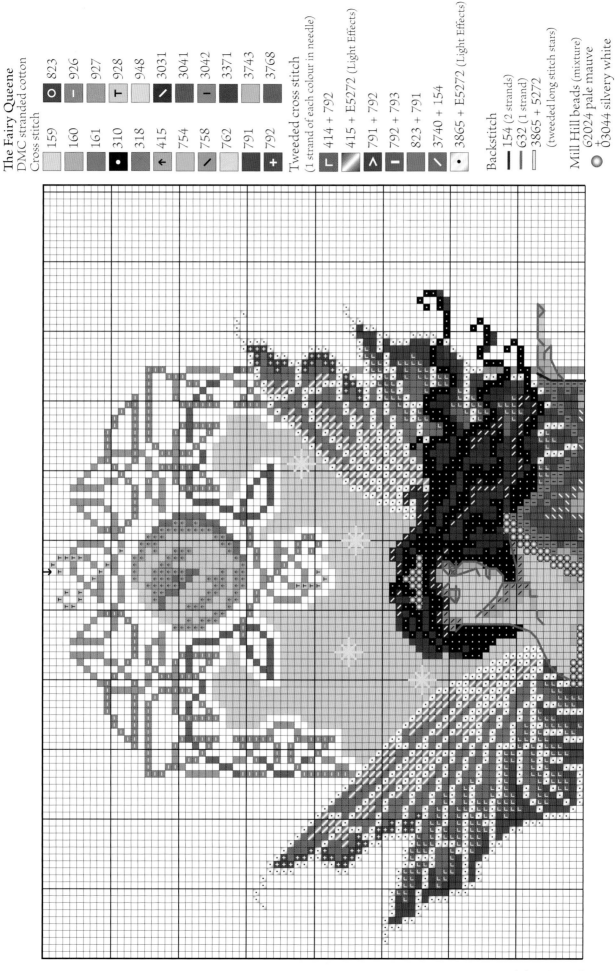

The Fairies are closely connected to the moon, some even altering their appearance with its phases. Fairy feasting and dancing often take place by the light of a full moon and fairies are said to travel on moonbeams.

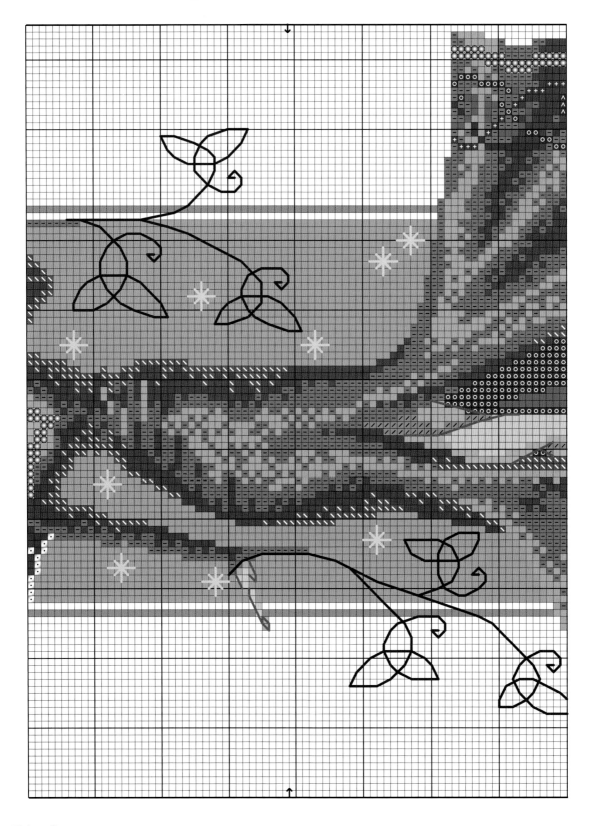

The Fairy Queene

DMC stranded cotton
Cross stitch

○	823	
I	926	
	927	
T	928	
	948	
╱	3031	
─	3041	
	3042	
	3371	
	3743	
	3768	

	159	
	160	
	161	
●	310	
	318	
←	415	
	754	
╱	758	
	762	
	791	
+	792	

Tweeded cross stitch
(1 strand of each colour in needle)

L	414 + 792	
╱	415 + E5272 (Light Effects)	
∧	791 + 792	
─	792 + 793	
╱	823 + 791	
•	3740 + 154	
	3865 + E5272 (Light Effects)	

Backstitch
—— 154 (2 strands)
| 632 (1 strand)
3865 + 5272
(tweeded long stitch stars)

Mill Hill beads (mixture)
● 62024 pale mauve
† 03044 silvery white

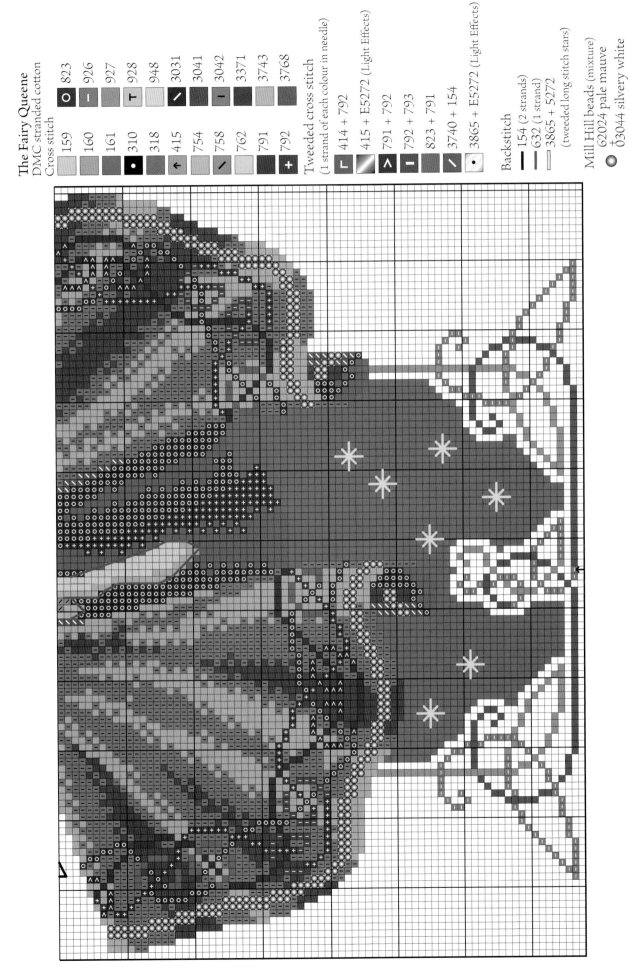

The Fairy Queene **67**

Wizard Magic

Legends and fairytales are full of stories of the magical power of wizards and they seem just as popular today, as this detailed design shows. The wizard is nowhere to be seen, but even in his absence weird and wonderful things are happening in his chambers. The wizard's quill is magically writing notes for his future invocations. His crystal ball glitters with mysterious omens and the cherished goblet promises to fulfil every fantasy. Feathered and furry friends peer from sheltered spots, curious as to when the wizard will return to cast more of his enchanting spells.

This colourful design reveals some of the mysterious paraphernalia of the master wizard's trade. Who knows what he might dream up for his next illusion?

Wizard Magic Picture

This interesting design is such fun to stitch. Like the wizard's chambers, it is crammed with magical motifs and the tools of his trade. It is worked on an unusual opalescent fabric, which adds a mystical glow to the design, while metallic threads bring an extra sparkle. It could also be worked on 14-count Aida.

Stitch count
168 x 138

Design size
30.5 x 25cm (12 x 9¾in)

Materials
43 x 38cm (17 x 15in) 28-count Jazlynn in opalescent white (Zweigart code 3626/011/55)

★

Tapestry needle size 24–26

★

DMC stranded cotton (floss) as listed in chart key

★

Kreinik Very Fine (#4) Braid: 002 gold, 045 confetti gold and 1432 blue ice

1 Prepare for work, referring to page 97 if necessary. Mark the centre of the fabric and the centre of the chart on pages 72–75. Mount fabric in an embroidery frame if you wish.

2 Start stitching from the centre of the chart and fabric, using two strands of stranded cotton (floss) for full and quarter cross stitches (for this chart, quarter stitches are shown by triangles). Then work the backstitch with two strands for colours 318 and 3837, and one strand for all other backstitch colours. Use one strand for all the Kreinik cross stitches and backstitches.

3 When the embroidery is complete, check for missed stitches and make up as a framed picture (see page 99).

Magical Makes

The owl and hourglass would be perfect for a bookmark for a hard-working student if you add the words 'Time flies when you're studying!' using the alphabet below. Stitch it on 28-count evenweave and work a backstitched line above and below the design and then fray the fabric edges.

Magical Makes

Why not stitch parts of this design to create smaller pictures? The cute black cat snoozing under the wizard's hat would make a fun little picture or a patch for a study notebook.

ABCDEFGHI
JKLMNOPQR
STUVWXYZ
abcdefghijklmn
opqrstuvwxyz
1234567890

Wizard Magic

DMC stranded cotton
Cross stitch

I 209	• 310	T 415	— 746	L 840	907		
211	318	+ 436	803	842	✔ 976		
300	349	676	✖ 826	895	905		
301	352	680	827	3837	• blanc		

Kreinik Very Fine (#4) Braid

002 gold

045 confetti gold

1432 blue ice

Backstitch

— 310

— 318 (2 strands)

— 3837 (2 strands)

▨▨ Kreinik 045 confetti gold

▨▨ Kreinik 1432 blue ice

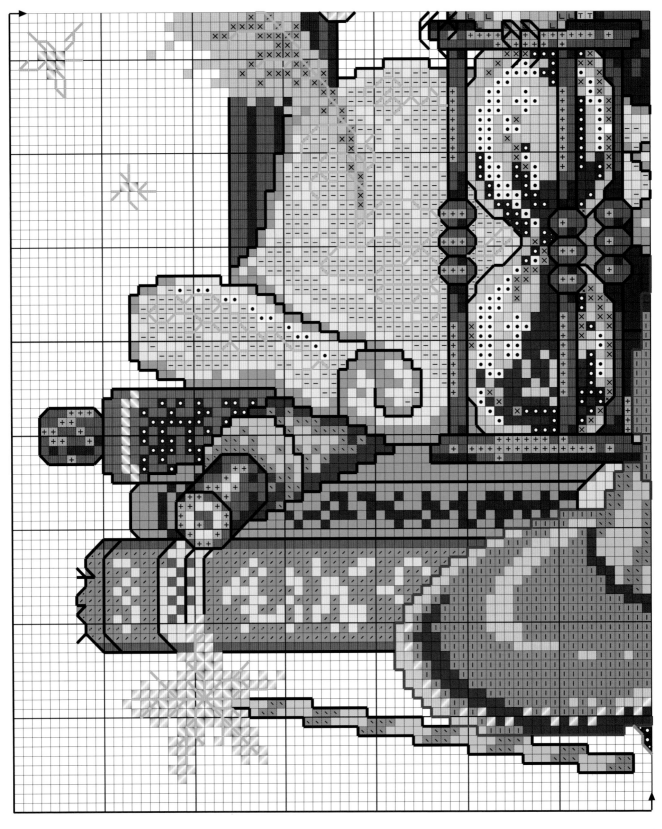

Wizard Magic

DMC stranded cotton
Cross stitch

I 209	• 310	T 415	− 746	L 840	907
211	318	+ 436	803	842	╱ 976
300	349	676	✕ 826	895	╲ 905
301	352	680	827	3837	• blanc

Kreinik Very Fine (#4) Braid

╱ 002 gold
╱ 045 confetti gold
╱ 1432 blue ice

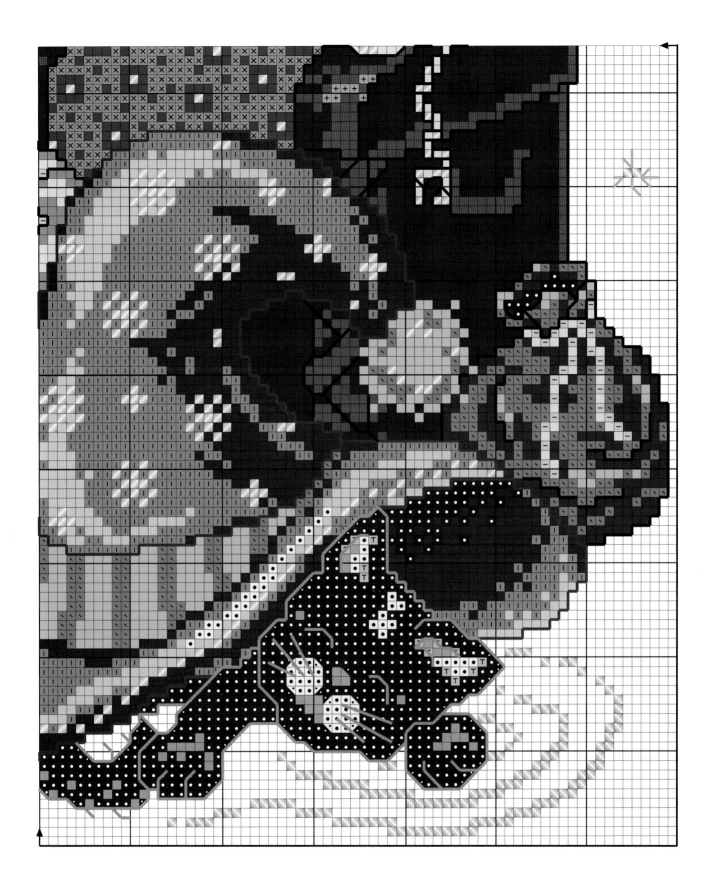

Backstitch

— 310

━━ 318 (2 strands)

— 3837 (2 strands)

━━ Kreinik 045 confetti gold

━━ Kreinik 1432 blue ice

Designed by Lesley Teare

Mermaid Enchantment

Stories of mermaids have been told for centuries in folklore,

legend and fairytales, and images of such

enchanted water sprites have appeared in art

as diverse as ancient Greek pottery and 21st-century

films. The traditional image of a mermaid is of a

mysterious and enticing maiden with the face and body

of a woman but with a fish tail instead of legs. Mermaids

are sometimes glimpsed sunning themselves on wave-washed rocks,

combing their long hair and admiring their reflection in pearly mirrors.

They may wear a seaweed crown and adorn themselves with pearls

and other treasures of the deep. This sweet mermaid is reminiscent

of Hans Christian Andersen's delightful yet tragic creation.

This lovely young mermaid is sure to enchant everyone. She gleams with iridescent metallic threads and is framed by a sea-theme border of shells, seahorses and tropical fish.

Mermaid Enchantment

At home in the sea, this mermaid's scales gleam with metallic threads. Movement is created by the bubbles rising from her fishy friends and her hair coiling like seaweed in the ocean currents. The design is stitched on ice blue Aida fabric for a watery atmosphere but could also be worked on linen. There are two smaller projects overleaf which use some of the motifs from the main chart.

Stitch count
187h x 159w
Design size
34 x 29cm (13½ x 11½in)

Materials
46 x 41cm (18 x 16in)
14-count Aida in ice blue
(Zweigart code 550)

★

Tapestry needle size 24–26
and a beading needle

★

DMC stranded cotton (floss)
as listed in chart key

★

Kreinik Very Fine (#4) braids
as listed in chart key

★

Mill Hill glass beads in pearl 00123

★

Suitable picture frame

1 Prepare for work, referring to page 97 if necessary. Mark the centre of the fabric and the centre of the chart on pages 82–85. Mount fabric in an embroidery frame if you wish.

2 Start stitching from the centre of the chart and fabric. Stitch over one block, working the full and three-quarter cross stitches with two strands of stranded cotton (floss) but only one strand when using the Kreinik #4 braids (see chart key). Work all backstitches with one strand of thread, stitching the stranded cotton backstitches first, then the metallic ones. Because of the number of colour changes it is a good idea to keep several needles threaded with different colours.

3 Using a beading needle and matching thread, attach the seed beads (see page 98) according to the positions shown on the chart.

4 When all the stitching is complete, remove from the embroidery frame. Press the work wrong side down on thick towels with a cool iron, taking extra care with the metallic threads and beads. You can now frame your work – see the instructions on page 99.

Magical Makes

You could create a height chart for a child's room by stitching individual motifs from the mermaid chart in a long shape like this. A scale, in either inches or centimetres, could be added up the side in simple backstitch numbers (see chart on page 70). Mount the finished piece on to stiff card and hang it on the wall.

In the past, sailors believed in mermaids and their power to enchant, confusing them with sirens, whose songs drew men to their doom. Ancient naval maps often had a drawing of a mermaid in the middle of the ocean with the warning words hic sunt sirenae (here be mermaids).

Seaside Towel Band

1 Find the centre of your strip of Aida and stitch the design from the centre outwards over one block. Follow the chart on page 85 and use the mermaid key (although you won't need all of the colours in the key). Work the cross stitches with two strands for the stranded cotton (floss) and one strand for the Kreinik thread.

Work the backstitches with one strand of stranded cotton. Repeat the design as necessary to suit your towel width.

2 When all the stitching is finished hem all edges of the Aida strip by 1.25cm (½in). Find the centre of the towel and the centre of the band and pin the band on to the towel. Slipstitch or machine into place and remove pins when finished.

Stitch count of motif
23h x 109w
Design size of motif
20 x 4cm (8 x 1¾in)

Materials
14-count Aida in ice blue (Zweigart code 550) 8.2cm (3¼in) high (includes turnings) x the width of your towel (plus turnings)

★

Tapestry needle size 24–26

★

DMC stranded cotton (floss) as listed in mermaid chart key

★

Kreinik Very Fine (#4) Braid 9192 light peach

★

Small guest or hand towel

Magical Makes

Use other motifs from the mermaid chart to stitch a variety of towel bands, perhaps working them on Aida bands with wavy edges to echo the watery theme. Alternatively, the fish and seahorses on their own would make a charming set of coasters.

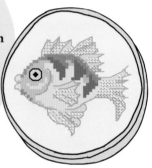

Seahorse Face Cloth

1 Stitch the seahorse motif from the main mermaid chart on page 83 on to the Aida.

2 Trim the stitched design, leaving enough of a border to make a fringe and then slipstitch the Aida piece on to the flannel. Fray the edges once it has been stitched firmly into place.

Stitch count of motif
32h x 17w
Design size of motif
6 x 3cm (2¼ x 1¼in)

Materials
12.5 x 10cm (5 x 4in) 14-count Aida in ice blue (Zweigart code 550)

★

Tapestry needle size 24–26

★

DMC stranded cotton (floss) as listed in mermaid chart key

★

Kreinik Very Fine (#4) Braid 032 pearl

★

Face cloth (flannel)

Magical Makes

Rearrange some of the design elements from the mermaid picture to create a door plate like this, leaving space for a child's name.

The colourful tropical fish, seahorses and shells that surround the mermaid are ideal for adorning all sorts of items and perfect for a bathroom setting.

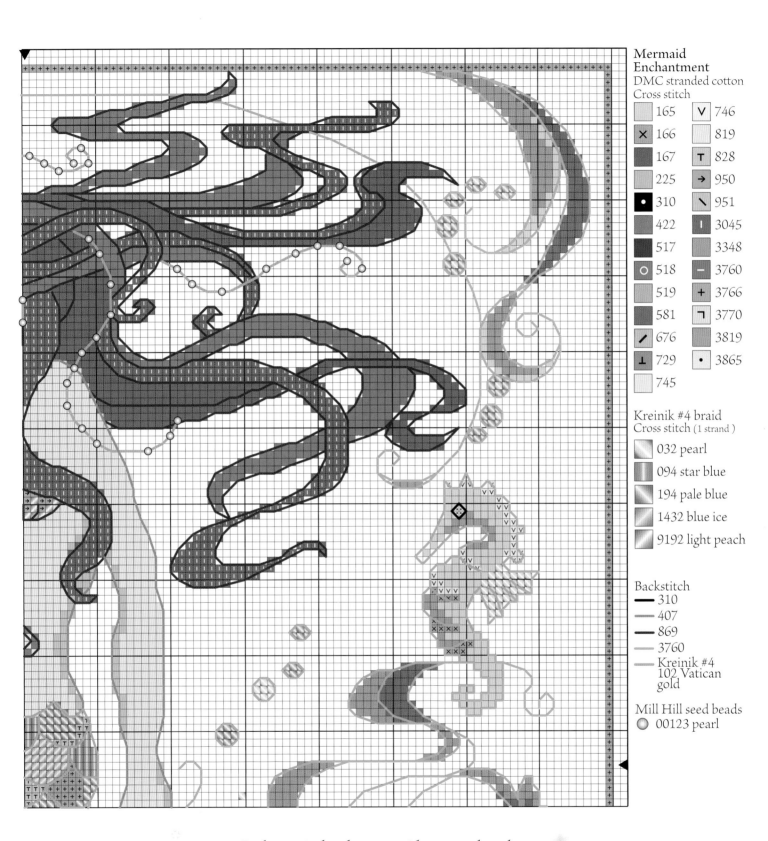

DMC stranded cotton
Cross stitch

165		V	746
×	166		819
	167	T	828
	225	→	950
⊙	310	\	951
	422	I	3045
	517	—	3348
O	518	–	3760
	519	+	3766
	581	⌐	3770
/	676		3819
⊥	729	•	3865
	745		

Kreinik #4 braid
Cross stitch (1 strand)

- 032 pearl
- 094 star blue
- 194 pale blue
- 1432 blue ice
- 9192 light peach

Backstitch
— 310
— 407
— 869
— 3760
⋯ Kreinik #4
102 Vatican
gold

Mill Hill seed beads
⊙ 00123 pearl

In the magical realm mermaids are not the only
water sprites: Nereids are nymphs of the sea,
Naiads are found in brooks and fountains,
Dryads inhabit woodland waters, while
Oreads favour mountain streams and grottos.

...Once I sat upon a promontory,
And heard a mermaid on a dolphin's back
Uttering such dulcet and harmonious breath
That the rude sea grew civil at her song,
And certain stars shot madly from their spheres
To hear the sea-maid's music.
(A Midsummer Night's Dream, William Shakespeare)

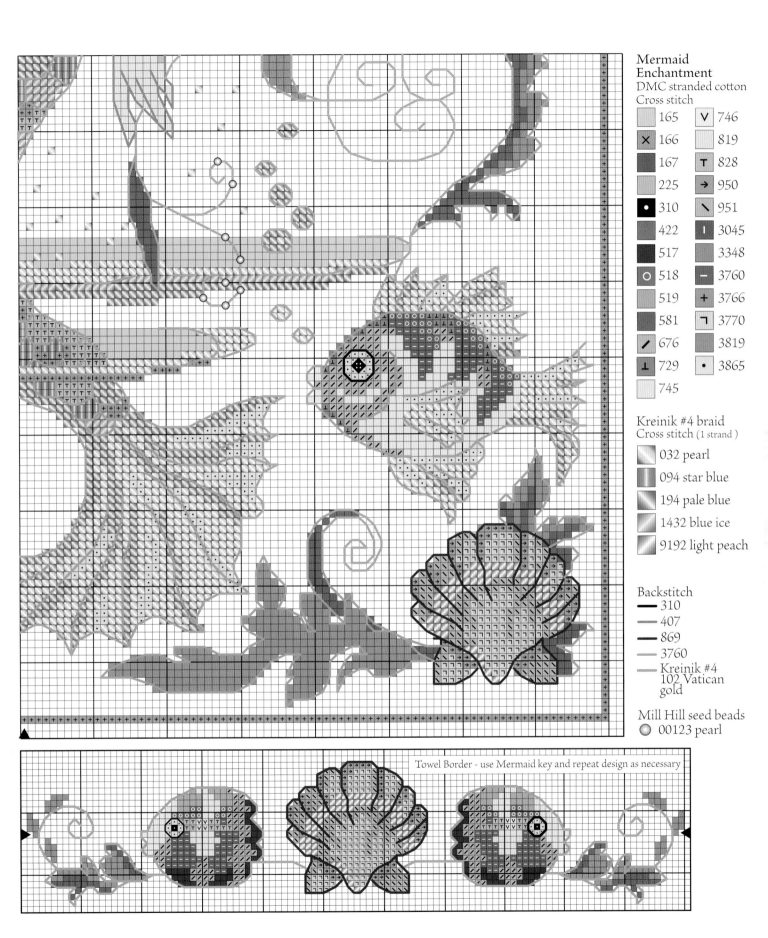

Mermaid Enchantment

DMC stranded cotton
Cross stitch

	165	V	746
×	166		819
	167	T	828
	225	→	950
⊙	310	\	951
	422	I	3045
	517		3348
O	518	—	3760
	519	+	3766
	581	⌐	3770
/	676		3819
⊥	729	•	3865
	745		

Kreinik #4 braid
Cross stitch (1 strand)

- 032 pearl
- 094 star blue
- 194 pale blue
- 1432 blue ice
- 9192 light peach

Backstitch
— 310
— 407
— 869
— 3760
— Kreinik #4 102 Vatican gold

Mill Hill seed beads
○ 00123 pearl

Towel Border - use Mermaid key and repeat design as necessary

Designed by Joanne Sanderson

Blooming Fairies

Fairies are linked to flowers of all sorts, natural companions and guardians that share common traits of beauty, delicacy and innocence. It is no wonder that artists have portrayed the natural world teeming with spirits such as fairies and elves. The artistic imaginations of Victorian painters in particular were fired by the world that diminutive fairies share with flowers, insects and birds.

These lovely designs give us a detailed look at the world of a flower fairy. In each of four flowers we find a pretty fairy friend. Dressed in delicate pinks, the rose fairy demurely poses in the heart of a full-blown rose. The youthful buttercup fairy rests on a perch of buttery yellows and golds. The poppy fairy sits pensively on crumpled petals of flamboyant red. The shy waterlily fairy nestles into the protective petals of her favourite flower.

These delightful flower fairies are simply magical. Their gauzy butterfly wings and diaphanous gowns glitter with fairy dust, while gold and pearl beads decorate their hair.

Rose Fairy

For thousands of years the rose has been the queen of flowers, associated with love and romance. This fairy drinks in its delicious scent, which is just as attractive to fairies as it is to us. All four flower fairy designs could be stitched on 28-count evenweave instead of Aida – worked over two fabric threads to give the same finished size.

Stitch count
94h x 93w
Design size
17 x 17cm (6¾ x 6¾in)

Materials
35 x 35cm (14 x 14in) 14-count Aida in off-white (DMC 712)

★

Tapestry needle size 24–26 and a beading needle

★

DMC stranded cotton (floss) as listed in chart key

★

DMC Light Effects threads as listed in chart key

★

Pearl or cream seed beads

★

Suitable picture frame with aperture approx 18 x 18cm (7 x 7in)

1 Prepare for work, referring to page 97 if necessary. Mark the centre of the fabric and the centre of the chart opposite.

2 Start stitching from the centre of the chart and fabric, working over one block of Aida (or two threads of evenweave) and using two strands of stranded cotton (floss) for full and three-quarter cross stitches and for French knots. Use one strand for backstitch. Use a beading needle and matching thread to sew on the beads (see page 98).

3 When all stitching is completed, remove from the embroidery frame. Press gently on the wrong side on a thick towel to prevent the stitches becoming flattened, taking care with beads and metallic threads. Frame your work following the instructions on page 99.

Magical Makes

Stitch any of the fairies on their flowers and make up into a sweet heart-shaped pillow or nightdress case for a little girl's room.

Rose Fairy

DMC stranded cotton

Cross stitch

156	604	987	3770	E818 (Light Effects)
434	777	989		E5200 (Light Effects)
436	801	3348		
600	948	3688		
602	963	3747		

Backstitch
— 600
— 801

French knots
● 801 (eyes)

Seed beads
◉ pearl or cream

Poppy Fairy

The red poppy is all sultry extravagance – from its flaming crimson-red colour to the huge size of its bowl-like blooms. This fairy is quite at home among the swelling seed pod and feathery purple-black stamens.

Stitch count
91h x 93w
Design size
16.5 x 17cm (6½ x 6¾in)

★

Materials
35 x 35cm (14 x 14in) 14-count
Aida in off-white (DMC 712)

★

Tapestry needle size 24–26
and a beading needle

★

DMC stranded cotton (floss)
as listed in chart key

★

DMC Light Effects threads
as listed in chart key

★

Gold seed beads

★

Suitable picture frame with aperture
approx 18 x 18cm (7 x 7in)

1 Prepare for work and stitch the Poppy Fairy in the same way as the Rose Fairy, following the relevant chart. Make up as a picture, as before.

Magical Makes

The flower fairy designs are more or less the same size, so they can be used interchangeably to decorate sets of items such as pictures, cushions and book covers. Why not combine them all into a spectacular wall hanging, choosing a plain or print fabric colour to border the designs? See page 54 for general instructions on making a hanging.

Poppy Fairy
DMC stranded cotton
Cross stitch

▨ 153	▌ 433	– 754	▓ 986	▨ E967 (Light Effects)
▨ 164	╱ 435	772	v 989	▨ E3821 (Light Effects)
▨ 352	✕ 498	▓ 801	3770	▨ E5200 (Light Effects)
⊙ 353	▨ 666	815	⊙ 3834	
▮ 369	• 712	╲ 966	+ 3836	

Backstitch
— 666
— 801

French knot
● 801 (eye)

Seed beads
⊙ gold

Buttercup Fairy

*The buttercup is one of the most well-known and loved wildflowers.
With its pure, sunny colour it is no wonder that it is used to symbolize
youth, energy and innocence, just like its pretty fairy companion.*

Stitch count
84h x 93w
Design size
15.5 x 17cm (6 x 6¾in)

Materials
35 x 35cm (14 x 14in)
14-count Aida in white
★
Tapestry needle size 24–26
and a beading needle
★
DMC stranded cotton (floss)
as listed in chart key
★
DMC Light Effects threads
as listed in chart key
★
Gold seed beads
★
Square box to fit embroidery
★
Double-sided adhesive tape
★
Decorative ribbon or braid
to trim, 1m (1yd)
★
Craft glue

1 Prepare for work, referring to page 97 if necessary. Mark the centre of the fabric and the centre of the chart opposite. Mount your fabric in an embroidery frame if you wish.

2 Start stitching from the centre of the chart and fabric, working over one block of Aida (or two threads of evenweave) and using two strands of stranded cotton (floss) for full and three-quarter cross stitches and one strand for backstitch. Use a beading needle and matching thread to sew on the beads (see page 98).

3 When all stitching is completed, remove from the embroidery frame. Press gently on the wrong side on to a thick towel. Trim the embroidery to the desired size and use double-sided tape to stick it to the top of the box ensuring the design is central. Finish by sticking or gluing ribbon or decorative braid around the design to conceal the edges and finish with a little bow.

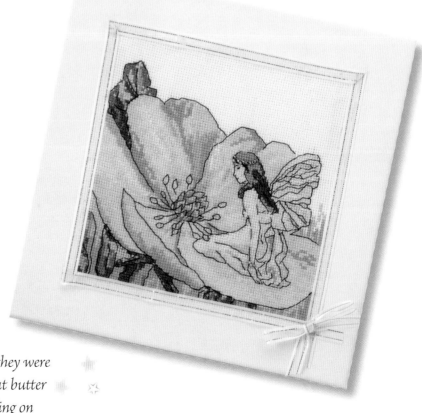

*Buttercups are so-called because they were
once thought to be the reason that butter
was so yellow, due to cows feeding on
buttercups while grazing in meadows.*

Buttercup Fairy

DMC stranded cotton

Cross stitch

I	164		745	\	989
	725	o	772		3348
/	726	V	948		3770
L	743		972		3826
—	744		987	•	3827

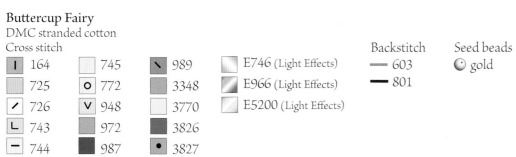

E746 (Light Effects)
E966 (Light Effects)
E5200 (Light Effects)

Backstitch
▬▬ 603
▬▬ 801

Seed beads
◉ gold

Waterlily Fairy

In the Victorian language of flowers the waterlily meant purity of heart because, like a chaste maiden (or fairy!), its flowers do not open until midday and then retire in early evening. This flower fairy looks very content in her comfortable bed of petals.

Stitch count
78h x 93w
Design size
14 x 17cm (5½ x 6¾in)

Materials
35 x 35cm (14 x 14in)
14-count Aida in white

★

Tapestry needle size 24–26
and a beading needle

★

DMC stranded cotton (floss)
as listed in chart key

★

DMC Light Effects threads
as listed in chart key

★

Pearl or cream seed beads

★

Ready-made cushion cover
35 x 35cm (14 x 14in)
or fabric to make a cover (step 3)

★

Iron-on fusible web

★

Decorative cord to trim

★

Polyester filling or cushion pad

1 Prepare for work, referring to page 97 if necessary. Mark the centre of the fabric and the centre of the chart opposite. Mount your fabric in an embroidery frame if you wish.

2 Start stitching from the centre of the chart and fabric, working over one block of Aida (or two threads of evenweave) and using two strands of stranded cotton (floss) for full and three-quarter cross stitches and for French knots. Use one strand for backstitch. Use a beading needle and matching thread to sew on the beads (see page 98).

3 When all stitching is completed, remove from the embroidery frame and press gently on the wrong side on a thick towel. If you prefer to make your own cushion cover see page 51 (steps 3–6) for general instructions.

To use a ready-made cover, begin by backing your finished embroidery with iron-on fusible web and trimming to the desired size. Fuse the embroidery on to the centre front of the cushion cover and then hand sew decorative cord all around the edge. Finish by knotting the cord and allowing the ends to unravel to make a little tassel.

Waterlily Fairy
DMC stranded cotton
Cross stitch

▨ 340	▨ 743	⌊ 948
◣ 341	▨ 745	▨ 963
▨ 603	− 772	▨ 3770
▮ 605	◿ 819	• blanc
▨ 703	▨ 910	

◩ E168 (Light Effects)	
◩ E818 (Light Effects)	
◩ E3747 (Light Effects)	

Backstitch
═══ 603
──── 801

French knots
● 801 (eyes)

Seed beads
☉ pearl or cream

The Latin name for waterlilies, Nymphe,
comes from the Greek water spirit and
goddess of springs, Nymphe, because the
flowers grew where nymphs liked to play.

Materials and Techniques

This section describes the materials and equipment you need to complete the projects in this book, followed by the basic techniques and stitches required. For beginners there are some handy tips on page 101 for perfect stitching.

Equipment

Very few materials, tools or items of equipment are needed for successful cross stitch embroidery.

Fabrics

The fabrics used for counted cross stitch, mainly Aidas and evenweaves, are woven with the same number of threads or blocks to 2.5cm (1in) in both directions. They are available in different counts – the higher the count, the more threads or stitches to 2.5cm (1in), and the finer the fabric.
Aida This is ideal for the beginner because the threads are woven in blocks rather than singly. It is available in many fibres, colours and counts and as different width bands. When stitching on Aida, one block on the fabric corresponds to one square on a chart and generally cross stitch is worked over *one block*.

Evenweaves These are made from various fibres including linen, cotton and acrylic. Evenweaves are woven singly and are available in different colours, counts and bands. To even out any oddities in the weave, cross stitch is usually worked over *two threads* of the fabric.

Threads

The most commonly used thread for counted embroidery is stranded cotton (floss). The DMC range has been used by the designers in this book but if you prefer to work with the Anchor range refer to the conversion table on page 102.

Some of the projects feature metallic threads to create a magical glitter: these include metallic braid (#4) from the Kreinik range and various metallic and pearlescent colours from the new DMC Light Effects range. These can be used alone for a shiny look or in combination with stranded cottons. Some Caron space-dyed threads are also used. The project instructions give how many strands of each thread to use.
Tweeding You can increase the number of thread colours in your palette by blending or tweeding – that is, combining two or more thread colours in your needle at the same time and working as one to achieve a mottled effect.

Beads

Many of the designs in the book use beads to bring an extra sparkle and dimension to the cross stitch. If you want to use beads as an embellishment there are many types and colours to choose from. Mill Hill glass seed beads and Magnifica beads were used in this book. See page 98 for how to attach beads.

Tools

There are many tools and gadgets available for embroidery in craft shops but you really only need the following.
Needles Use blunt tapestry needles for counted cross stitch. The most common sizes used are 24 and 26 but the size depends on the project you are working on and personal preference. Avoid leaving a needle in the fabric unless it is gold plated or it may cause marks. A beading needle (or fine 'sharp' needle), which is much thinner and longer, will be needed to attach seed beads.
Scissors Use a pair of sharp dressmaker's shears for cutting fabric and a small, sharp pair of pointed scissors for cutting embroidery threads.
Frames and hoops These are not essential but if you use one, choose one large enough to hold the complete design to avoid marking the fabric and flattening your stitches.

Basic Techniques

The following pages describe the basic techniques you will need – how to prepare fabric for work, how to use the charts and keys and how to work the stitches.

Preparing Fabric for Work
Press embroidery fabric before you begin stitching and trim the selvedge or rough edges. Work from the middle of the fabric and middle of the chart to ensure your design is centred on the fabric. Find the middle of fabric by folding it in four and pressing lightly. Mark the folds with tailor's chalk or tacking (basting) stitches following a fabric thread. When working with linen sew a hem around all raw edges to preserve them for finishing later.

Stitch Count and Design Size
Each project gives details of the stitch count and finished design size but if you wish to work the design on a different count fabric you will need to be able to calculate the finished size. Count the number of stitches in the design and divide this by the fabric count number, e.g., 140 stitches x 140 stitches ÷ by 14-count = a design size of 10 x 10in (25.4 x 25.4cm). Remember that working on evenweave usually means working over two threads not one, so divide the fabric count by two before you start.

Using the Charts
The designs in this book are worked from colour charts, with symbols where necessary. Each square, both occupied and unoccupied, represents two threads of linen or one block of Aida. Each occupied square equals one stitch. Some designs use three-quarter cross stitches, shown as a triangle within a grid square. Some designs use French knots and beads and these are labelled in the key.

Starting and Finishing Stitching
Unless indicated otherwise, begin stitching in the middle of a design to ensure an adequate margin for making up. Start and finish stitching neatly, avoiding knots which can create lumps.

Knotless loop start This neat start can be used with an even number of strands i.e., 2, 4 or 6. To stitch with two strands, begin with one strand about 80cm (30in).

Double it and thread the needle with the two ends. Put the needle up through the fabric from the wrong side, where you intend to begin stitching, leaving the loop at the back. Form a half cross stitch, put the needle back through the fabric and through the waiting loop. The stitch is now anchored and you can begin.

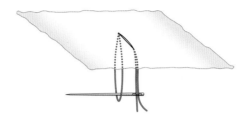

A knotless loop start

Away waste knot start Start this way if using an odd number of strands or when tweeding threads. Thread your needle with the number of strands required and knot the end. Insert the needle into the right side of the fabric about 2.5cm (1in) from where you wish to begin stitching. Stitch towards the knot and cut it off when the threads are anchored. Alternatively, snip off the knot, thread the needle and work under a few stitches to anchor.

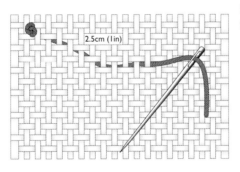

An away waste knot start

Finishing stitching At the back of the work, pass the needle and thread under several stitches of the same or similar colour, and then snip off the loose end close to the stitching. You can begin a new colour in a similar way.

Finishing off

Working the Stitches

The projects in the book use basic counted stitches that are easy to work: simply follow the instructions and diagrams below and overleaf.

Backstitch
Backstitch is used for outlining a design or part of a design, to add detail or emphasis, or for lettering. It is added after the cross stitch has been completed so the backstitch line isn't broken by cross stitches. It is shown on charts by solid coloured lines.

Follow the numbered sequence in the diagram below, working the stitches over one block of Aida or over two threads of evenweave, unless stated otherwise on the chart.

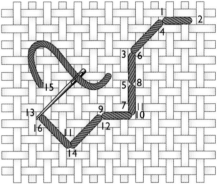

Backstitch

Cross Stitch
This is the most commonly used stitch in this book and it can be worked singly, where a whole cross stitch is created (see diagram overleaf), or in two journeys. For neat stitching, keep the top stitch facing the same direction. Half cross stitch is simply a single diagonal line.

Cross stitch on Aida Cross stitch on Aida fabric is normally worked over one block of the fabric. To work a complete cross stitch, follow the numbered sequence in the diagram overleaf: bring the needle up through the fabric at 1, cross one block of the fabric and insert the needle at 2. Push the needle through and bring it up at 3, ready to complete the stitch at 4. To continue on and work the adjacent stitch, bring the needle up at the bottom right-hand corner of the first stitch.

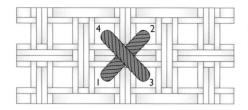

Single cross stitch on Aida fabric

To work cross stitches in two journeys, work the first leg of the cross stitch as above but instead of completing the stitch, work the adjacent half stitch and continue on to the end of the row. Complete all the crosses by working the other diagonals on the return journey.

Cross stitch in two journeys on Aida fabric

Cross stitch on evenweave Cross stitch on evenweave is usually worked over two threads of the fabric in each direction to even out any oddities in the thickness of the fibres. Bring the needle up to the left of a vertical thread to make it easier to spot counting mistakes. Work your cross stitch in two directions, in a sewing movement, half cross stitch in one direction and then work back and cover the original stitches with the second row. This forms neat, single vertical lines on the back and gives somewhere to finish raw ends.

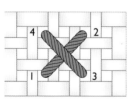

Single cross stitch on evenweave

Three-quarter Cross Stitch

Three-quarter cross stitch is a fractional stitch which can produce the illusion of curves. The stitch can be formed on either Aida or evenweave but is more successful on evenweave. They are shown on charts as a half square triangle (see diagram).

Work the first half of a cross stitch as usual. Work the second 'quarter' stitch

over the top and down into the central hole to anchor the first half of the stitch. If using Aida, you will need to push the needle through the centre of a block of the fabric. Where two three-quarter stitches lie back-to-back in the space of one full cross stitch, work both of the respective quarter stitches into the central hole.

Three-quarter cross stitches on evenweave

French Knot

French knots are small but important little stitches that are predominantly used for eyes and to add detail to a design. They are shown on the charts as coloured circles, with the thread code in the key.

Bring the needle through to the front of the fabric and wind the thread around the needle twice. Begin to push the needle partly through to the back, one thread or part of a block away from the entry point. (This will stop the stitch being pulled to the wrong side.) Gently pull the thread you have wound so it sits snugly at the point where the needle enters the fabric. Pull the needle through to the back and you should have a perfect knot in position. For bigger French knots, it is best to add more strands of thread to the needle rather than winding more times.

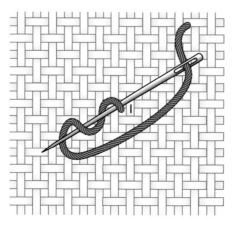

Starting to form a French knot

Completing a French knot

Long Stitch

Long straight stitches are used in some of the designs. They are very simple to stitch and can be worked on any fabric. On some designs long stitches are worked to create a star, for example The Fairy Queene on page 60. To work long stitch, simply bring the needle and thread up where the stitch is to start, at 1 in the diagram below, and down where the chart indicates it should finish, at 2.

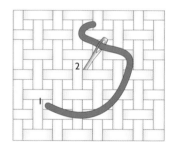

Long stitch

Attaching Beads

Seed beads make a wonderful embellishment to cross stitch and are especially effective for the magical designs in this book. Beads are shown on the charts as a large coloured circle, with details of the bead type and code in the key. Attach beads using a beading needle or very fine 'sharp' needle, thread that matches the bead colour and a half cross stitch (or a full cross stitch if you prefer).

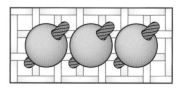

Attaching beads

Making Up

The cross stitch designs in this book have been made up in different ways – as pictures, cushions, wall hangings and box tops. In general, the instructions are given within the projects, with some common methods described here. There are also many 'Magical Makes' throughout the book, giving ideas for other ways to use the designs and display your work.

Mounting Work in Cards

Many of the smaller designs in the book would make great greetings cards – see the Butterfly Card below and the Celtic Card on page 64. There are many card blanks available from craft shops and mail-order suppliers (see page 103) and you can also make your own cards.

Making a Double-Fold Card with Aperture

1 Choose a card colour to complement your embroidery (for the butterfly card this was pearlized azure blue card) and cut a piece 30 x 12cm (12 x 4¾in) as shown in the diagram below. On the wrong side of the card, draw two lines dividing it into three sections of 10cm (4in). Score gently along each line with the back of a craft knife to make folding easier.

2 In the centre section, mark an aperture slightly bigger than the finished size of the design; in the case of the butterfly an aperture of 5.7 x 5.7cm (2¼ x 2¼in), leaving a border of about 2.2cm (⅞in) along the top and sides. Cut out the aperture with a sharp craft knife, carefully cutting into the corners neatly. Trim the left edge of the first section by 2mm (⅛in) so that it lies flat when folded over to the inside of the card. This will cover the back of the stitching. Fold the left and then the right section on the scored lines.

Mounting Work into a Double-Fold Card

1 Lay the card right side up on top of the design so the stitching is centred in the aperture. Place a pin in each corner and remove the card. Trim the fabric to within about 1.5cm (⅝in) so it fits into the card.

2 On the wrong side of the card, stick double-sided tape around the aperture and peel off the backing tape. Place the card over the design, using the pins to guide it into position. Press down firmly so the fabric is stuck securely to the card.

3 On the wrong side of the card, stick tape around the middle section. Peel off the backing tape and fold the left section in to cover the back of the stitching, pressing down firmly.

Mounting Work on a Single-Fold Card

You can also mount your embroidery on a single-fold card. Trim your embroidery to the size required leaving two or three extra rows all round if you want a frayed edge. Pull away the outer fabric threads to fray and use double-sided tape to attach the embroidery to the front of your card.

Mounting and Framing a Picture

There are many stunning pictures in the book. You could take your work to a professional framer or mount the work yourself, using the following instructions, and then put it into a ready-made frame.

Materials
- Suitable picture frame
- Mount board the same size as the frame
- Wadding (batting)
- Double-sided adhesive tape
- Pins
- Crochet cotton or strong thread

1 Cut mount board to the size of the picture frame aperture. Cut wadding (batting) the same size and secure to the mount board with double-sided tape. Lay the embroidery face up on the wadding and when happy with the position, push a line of pins down each side into the board. Check the stitching is straight and then trim the fabric to leave 5cm (2in) all round.

2 Fold the excess fabric to the back. Thread a needle with strong thread, knot the end and lace the two opposite sides together on the back, starting at one end and working in a zigzag manner. Pull the lacing tight and adjust the laced threads one by one before finishing off. Repeat this process on the two remaining edges.

3 Fold down and stitch the corners. Remove pins and assemble in its picture frame.

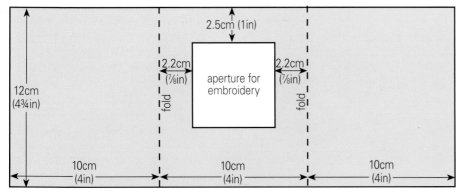

Making a double-fold aperture card

Making Up as a Drawstring Bag

Cross stitch designs are perfect for adorning bags. These instructions are for the drawstring bag on page 17.

Materials
- Background fabric for bag 0.25m (¼yd)
- Lightweight iron-on interfacing or thin wadding 0.25m (¼yd)
- Fusible web 0.25m (¼yd)
- Narrow satin ribbon 1m (1yd)
- Four small satin roses
- Permanent fabric glue

1 Cut two pieces of fabric 18 x 23cm (7 x 9in) and place right sides together. Leaving 7.6cm (3in) open at the top on both sides, stitch 1.25cm (½in) from the raw edges down one side, along the bottom, and up the other side. Trim bottom corners diagonally and press seams open. Turn the top edge over 4cm (1½in) to make a hem and a channel for the ribbon. Machine stitch a line 2cm (¾in) from the folded edge and another 1cm (⅜in) further down. Turn right side out.

2 Trim the embroidery to within six rows of the border. Cut interfacing the same size and fuse to the wrong side of the embroidery. Place fusible web the same size on the wrong side of the embroidery, making sure that the edges do not overlap, and fuse to the front of the bag. Glue narrow ribbon strips around the embroidery, gluing on a rose at each corner to cover the joins. Feed ribbon through the channel as a tie to finish.

Making Up as a Journal

There are many notebooks, diaries and journals that can be decorated with cross stitch designs. These instructions are for the journal on page 17 but the sizes given could be changed to fit other book sizes.

Materials
- A journal, approx 15 x 20cm (6 x 8in)
- Background fabric 0.5m (½yd)
- Lightweight iron-on interfacing or thin wadding 0.25m (¼yd)
- Fusible fleece and fusible web 0.5m (½yd) each
- Decorative trim 0.5m (½yd)
- Four satin roses
- Permanent fabric glue

1 Place the open journal on top of the cover fabric. Mark 5cm (2in) from the side edges of the journal and 10cm (4in) from top and bottom and cut the fabric. Cut fusible fleece to the same size as this fabric. Fuse the fleece to the wrong side of the cover fabric. Fold over 6mm (¼in) to the wrong side along all raw edges and stitch in place.

2 Using the journal as a measure, fold the top and bottom edges to meet the top and bottom edges of the journal. Press in place. Centre the opened journal on the cover fabric and fold the side edges towards the centre over the front and back covers creating pockets. Press the folds in place. Secure the undersides of these pockets with tacking (basting) stitches.

3 Trim the embroidery to within six rows of the border edge. Cut lightweight interfacing to the same size and fuse it to the wrong side of the embroidery. Place a piece of fusible web the same size on the wrong side of the embroidery, making sure that the edges do not overlap. Fold the cover in half and position the embroidery. Press to fuse the embroidery and background fabric together.

4 Glue decorative trim around the outer edge of the embroidery beginning and ending at the upper right corner. Glue a satin rose at each corner to finish.

Making Up as a Sachet

The solar design on page 9 has been made up into a scented sachet. The instructions that follow could also be used for other designs in the book.

Materials
- Backing fabric to tone with embroidery
- Short length of narrow ribbon for a hanging loop
- Decorative cord or ribbon
- Caron Wildflowers variegated thread 017 blue lavender for a tassel
- Pot-pourri

1 Trim the completed embroidery to the required size and cut a matching piece of backing fabric. With right sides together stitch the two pieces together, leaving a gap for turning at the top. Turn through to the right side and stuff with pot-pourri or polyester stuffing.

2 Slipstitch decorative cord or ribbon all around the edges of the sachet starting at the gap. Tuck the ends of the cord into the gap, add a hanging loop of narrow ribbon and then slipstitch the gap closed.

3 Sew a tassel to the centre bottom of the sachet (see panel opposite for making a tassel). There are also many decorative buttons that could be used for an extra finishing touch.

Making Up as a Wall Hanging

The following instructions are for the little wall hanging on page 18 but could be amended for a larger cross stitch design.

Materials
- Two 15 x 15cm (6 x 6in) squares of felt
- Lightweight iron-on interfacing or thin wadding 0.25m (¼yd)
- Fusible fleece and fusible web 0.25m (¼yd) each
- Decorative satin cord 1.25m (1¼yd)
- Four small satin roses and one decorative button
- Permanent fabric glue

1 Fuse a piece of felt and fusible fleece together. Layer the prepared felt, fleece side up, a piece of fusible web the same size, and the second piece of felt. Leaving the top edge open, use a press cloth to fuse the layers. For a decorative effect, use pinking shears to decorate the edge of the felt. Cut two 25.4cm (10in) lengths of satin cord and position them inside the open edge 2.5cm (1in) from either side. Press to fuse the top edge.

2 Trim the finished embroidery to within five rows of the border edge. Cut a piece of interfacing to the same size and fuse to the wrong side of the embroidery. Cut fusible web to the same size and place on the wrong side of the embroidery, making sure that the edges do not overlap the trimmed embroidery.

3 Centre the embroidery on the felt and fuse to the square. Glue the satin cord around the edge of the patch beginning and ending at the centre bottom. Glue a satin rose at each corner and a decorative button at the bottom to finish.

Making a Tassel

A tassel makes a nice finishing touch, for example on the corners of a cushion or sachet or at the end of a bookmark.

1 To make a simple tassel, cut a rectangular piece of stiff card, about 1.5cm (½in) longer than the desired size of the tassel. Choose a thread colour to match your project and wrap the thread repeatedly around the card to the desired thickness.

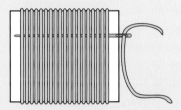

2 Slip a length of thread through the top of the tassel bundle and tie in a knot. Cut the threads at the bottom of the tassel bundle and slide the threads off the piece of card.

3 Now bind the top third of the tassel with another length of thread to form a 'neck'. Finally, trim all the tassel ends neatly to the same length.

Perfect Stitching

Organize your threads before you start a project as this will help to avoid confusion later. Put threads on an organizer (available from craft shops) and always include the manufacturer's name and the shade number.

Separate the strands on a skein of stranded cotton (floss) before taking the number you need, realigning them and threading your needle. This will help the threads to lie flat.

When stitching with metallic threads, work with shorter lengths, about 30cm (12in); this will not only help to avoid tangling but also reduce excessive wear on the thread.

If using an embroidery frame, try to avoid a hoop as it will stretch the fabric and leave a mark that may be difficult to remove.

If you do use a hoop or frame, use one large enough to house the whole design.

Plan your route carefully around the chart, counting over short distances where possible to avoid making counting mistakes.

Work your cross stitch in two directions in a sewing movement – half cross stitch in one direction and then cover those original stitches with the second row. This forms vertical lines on the back and gives somewhere to finish off raw ends tidily. For neat work the top stitches should all face the same direction.

★

When adding a backstitch outline, always add it after the cross stitch has been completed as this will prevent the solid line of the backstitch being broken. Resist the temptation to make your backstitches too long.

DMC –Anchor Thread Conversion

The designs in this book use DMC stranded cotton (floss). This DMC/Anchor thread conversion chart is only a guide, as exact colour comparisons cannot always be made. An asterisk * indicates an Anchor shade that has been used more than once so take care to avoid duplication in a design. If you wish to use Madeira threads, telephone for a conversion chart on 01765 640003 or email: acts@madeira.co.uk

DMC	Anchor	DMC	Anchor	DMC	Anchor	DMC	Anchor	DMC	Anchor	DMC	Anchor	DMC	Anchor	DMC	Anchor
B5200	1	355	1014	604	55	781	308*	912	209	3023	899	3765	170	3846	1090
white	2	356	1013*	605	1094	782	308*	913	204	3024	388*	3766	167	3847	1076*
ecru	387*	367	216	606	334	783	307	915	1029	3031	905*	3768	779	3848	1074*
150	59	368	214	608	330*	791	178	917	89	3032	898*	3770	1009	3849	1070*
151	73	369	1043	610	889	792	941	918	341	3033	387*	3772	1007	3850	188*
152	969	370	888*	611	898*	793	176*	919	340	3041	871	3773	1008	3851	186*
153	95*	371	887*	612	832	794	175	920	1004	3042	870	3774	778	3852	306*
154	873	372	887*	613	831	796	133	921	1003*	3045	888*	3776	1048*	3853	1003*
155	1030*	400	351	632	936	797	132	922	1003*	3046	887*	3777	1015	3854	313
156	118*	402	1047*	640	393	798	146	924	851	3047	887	3778	1013*	3855	311*
157	120*	407	914	642	392	799	145	926	850	3051	845*	3779	868	3856	347
158	178	413	236*	644	391	800	144	927	849	3052	844	3781	1050	3857	936*
159	120*	414	235*	645	273	801	359	928	274	3053	843	3782	388*	3858	1007
160	175*	415	398	646	8581*	806	169	930	1035	3064	883	3787	904*	3859	914*
161	176	420	374	647	1040	807	168	931	1034	3072	397	3790	904*	3860	379*
162	159*	422	372	648	900	809	130	932	1033	3078	292	3799	236*	3861	378
163	877	433	358	666	46	813	161*	934	852*	3325	129	3801	1098	3862	358*
164	240*	434	310	676	891	814	45	935	861	3326	36	3802	1019*	3863	379*
165	278*	435	365	677	361*	815	44	936	846	3328	1024	3803	69	3864	376
166	280*	436	363	680	901*	816	43	937	268*	3340	329	3804	63*	3865	2*
167	375*	437	362	699	923*	817	13*	938	381	3341	328	3805	62*	3866	926*
168	274*	444	291	700	228	818	23*	939	152*	3345	268*	3806	62*	48	1207
169	849*	445	288	701	227	819	271	943	189	3346	267*	3807	122	51	1220*
208	110	451	233	702	226	820	134	945	881	3347	266*	3808	1068	52	1209*
209	109	452	232	703	238	822	390	946	332	3348	264	3809	1066*	57	1203*
210	108	453	231	704	256*	823	152*	947	330*	3350	77	3810	1066*	61	1218*
211	342	469	267*	712	926	824	164	948	1011	3354	74	3811	1060	62	1202*
221	897*	470	266*	718	88	825	162*	950	4146	3362	263	3812	188	67	1212
223	895	471	265	720	326	826	161*	951	1010	3363	262	3813	875*	69	1218*
224	895	472	253	721	324	827	160	954	203*	3364	261	3814	1074	75	1206*
225	1026	498	1005	722	323*	828	9159	955	203*	3371	382	3815	877*	90	1217*
300	352	500	683	725	305*	829	906	956	40*	3607	87	3816	876*	91	1211
301	1049*	501	878	726	295*	830	277*	957	50	3608	86	3817	875*	92	1215*
304	19	502	877*	727	293	831	277*	958	187	3609	85	3818	923*	93	1210*
307	289	503	876*	729	890	832	907*	959	186	3685	1028	3819	278	94	1216
309	42	504	206*	730	845*	833	874*	961	76*	3687	68	3820	306	95	1209*
310	403	517	162*	731	281*	834	874*	962	75*	3688	75*	3821	305*	99	1204
311	148	518	1039	732	281*	838	1088	963	23*	3689	49	3822	295*	101	1213*
312	979	519	1038	733	280	839	1086	964	185	3705	35*	3823	386	102	1209*
315	1019*	520	862*	734	279	840	1084	966	240	3706	33*	3824	8*	103	1210*
316	1017	522	860	738	361*	841	1082	970	925	3708	31	3825	323*	104	1217*
317	400	523	859	739	366	842	1080	971	316*	3712	1023	3826	1049*	105	1218*
318	235*	524	858	740	316*	844	1041	972	298	3713	1020	3827	311	106	1203*
319	1044*	535	401	741	304	869	375	973	290	3716	25	3828	373	107	1203*
320	215	543	933	742	303	890	218	975	357	3721	896	3829	901*	108	1220*
321	47	550	101*	743	302	891	35*	976	1001	3722	1027	3830	5975	111	1218*
322	978	552	99	744	301	892	33*	977	1002	3726	1018	3831	29	112	1201*
326	59*	553	98	745	300	893	27	986	246	3727	1016	3832	28	113	1210*
327	101*	554	95	746	275	894	26	987	244	3731	76*	3833	31*	114	1213*
333	119	561	212	747	158	895	1044*	988	243	3733	75*	3834	100*	115	1206*
334	977	562	210	754	1012	898	380	989	242	3740	872	3835	98*	121	1210*
335	40*	563	208	758	9575	899	38	991	1076	3743	869	3836	90	122	1215*
336	150	564	206*	760	1022	900	333	992	1072	3746	1030	3837	100*	124	1210*
340	118	580	924	761	1021	902	897*	993	1070	3747	120	3838	177	125	1213*
341	117*	581	281*	762	234	904	258	995	410	3750	1036	3839	176*	126	1209*
347	1025	597	1064	772	259*	905	257	996	433	3752	1032	3840	120*		
349	13*	598	1062	775	128	906	256*	3011	856	3753	1031	3841	159*		
350	11	600	59*	776	24	907	255	3012	855	3755	140	3842	164*		
351	10	601	63*	778	968	909	923*	3013	853	3756	1037	3843	1089*		
352	9	602	57	779	380*	910	230	3021	905*	3760	162*	3844	410*		
353	8*	603	62*	780	309	911	205	3022	8581*	3761	928	3845	1089*		

Suppliers

When writing to suppliers for information or catalogues, remember to include a stamped, self-addressed envelope.

UK

Coats Crafts UK
PO Box 22, Lingfield House, McMullen Road, Darlington, County Durham DL1 1YQ
tel: 01325 394200 (consumer helpline)
www.coatscrafts.co.uk
For Anchor stranded cotton (floss) and other embroidery supplies (Coats also supply some Charles Craft products)

Craft Creations Ltd
Ingersoll House, Delamare Road, Cheshunt, Hertfordshire EN8 9HD
tel: 01992 781900
www.craftcreations.com
For greetings card blanks and card-making accessories

DMC Creative World
Pullman Road, Wigston, Leicestershire LE18 2DY
tel: 0116 281 1040
fax: 0116 281 3592
www.dmc/cw.com
For DMC stranded cotton (floss) and Light Effects threads, embroidery fabrics and needlework supplies

Framecraft Miniatures Ltd
Unit 3, Isis House, Lindon Road, Brownhills, West Midlands WS8 7BW
tel/fax (UK): 01543 360842
tel (international): 44 1543 373076
email: sales@framecraft.com
www.framecraft.com
For Mill Hill beads, buttons, charms, wooden and ceramic trinket pots, handbag mirrors, notebook covers and many other pre-finished items with cross stitch inserts

Impress Cards & Craft Materials
Slough Farm, Westhall, Halesworth, Suffolk IP19 8RN
tel: 01986 781422
www.impresscards.com
For greetings card blanks, card-making accessories and craft materials

Paper Cellar Ltd
Parkville House, Red Lion Parade, Pinner, Middlesex HA5 3RR
tel: 08718 713711
www.papercellar.com
For all sorts of craft papers and card

Willow Fabrics
95 Town Lane, Mobberley, Knutsford, Cheshire WA16 7HH
tel freephone (UK): 0800 0567811
(elsewhere): #44 (0) 1565 87 2225
www.willowfabrics.com
For embroidery fabrics and Madeira threads

USA

Charles Craft Inc.
PO Box 1049, Laurenburg, NC 28353
tel: 910 844 3521
email: ccraft@carolina.net
www.charlescraft.com
Cross stitch fabrics and many useful pre-finished items

Coats and Clark
PO Box 12229, Greenville, SC 29612–0229
tel: (800) 648 1479
www.coatsandclark.com
For Anchor stranded cotton (floss) and other embroidery supplies

Design Works Crafts Inc
170 Wilbur Place, Bohemia, NY 11716
tel: 631 244 5749
fax: 631 244 6138
email: customerservice@designworkscrafts.com
For card mounts and cross stitch kits of Joan Elliott designs

Mill Hill, a division of Wichelt Imports Inc.
N162 Hwy 35, Stoddard, WI 54658
tel: 608 788 4600
fax: 608 788 6040
email: millhill@millhill.com
www.millhill.com
For Mill Hill beads and a US source for Framecraft products

Kreinik Manufacturing Company Inc.
3106 Timanus Lane, Suite 101, Baltimore, MD 21244
tel: 1800 537 2166
email: kreinik@kreinik.com
www.kreinik.com
For a wide range of metallic threads and blending filaments

The WARM Company
954 East Union Street, Seattle, WA 98122
tel: 1 800 234 WARM
www.warmcompany.com
UK Distributor: W. Williams & Sons Ltd
tel: 020 7263 7311
For polyester filling, cotton wadding (batting) and Steam-a-Seam fusible web

Zweigart/Joan Toggit Ltd
262 Old Brunswick Road, Suite E, Piscataway, NJ 08854-3756
tel: 732 562 8888
email: info@zweigart.com
www.zweigart.com
For a large selection of cross stitch fabrics and pre-finished table linens

About the Designers

Claire Crompton

Claire studied knitwear design at college before joining the design team at DMC, and finally going freelance. Claire's work has appeared in several magazines, including *Cross Stitch Magic*. Her designs feature in many D&C books, including *Cross Stitch Greetings Cards*, *Cross Stitch Alphabets*, *Cross Stitch Angels* and in her solo books, *Cross Stitch Card Collection* and *Picture Your Pet in Cross Stitch*. Claire lives in the Tamar valley, Cornwall, UK.

Joan Elliott

Joan's creations have been enchanting cross stitch enthusiasts the world over for years and she is a leading artist for Design Works Crafts Inc. Her debut book for D&C, *A Cross Stitcher's Oriental Odyssey* was followed by *Cross Stitch Teddies*, *Cross Stitch Sentiments and Sayings* and *Native American Cross Stitch*. She is currently working on her next book. Joan divides her time between New York and Vermont, USA.

Ursula Michael

For over 20 years, Ursula has been delighting cross stitchers with her colourful, whimsical designs, which have appeared in needlecraft magazines, books, kits and home decorating accessories. Combining her love of needlework with an eye for decorative design, she has taken graphic art training, and needle and thread, down many avenues. She lives in Rhode Island, USA.

Joanne Sanderson

Joanne started designing cross stitch when a friend asked her to produce a chart. Soon afterwards she won a design competition in the *World of Cross Stitch* magazine and has been designing ever since. She now contributes to many needlecraft magazines including *Cross Stitcher*, *Cross Stitch Collection* and *Quick & Easy Cross Stitch* and produces designs for DMC kits. Joanne lives in Yorkshire, UK, with her husband and daughter.

Lesley Teare

Lesley trained as a textile designer, with a degree in printed and woven textiles. For years she has been one of DMC's leading designers and her designs have featured in many cross stitch magazines. Lesley has contributed designs to numerous books for D&C, including *Cross Stitch Greetings Cards*, *Cross Stitch Angels* and *Cross Stitch Fairies*, as well as her solo books, *101 Weekend Cross Stitch Gifts* and *Travel the World in Cross Stitch*.

Carol Thornton

Carol has had a varied career but has always been deeply involved with arts and crafts, including photography, carpet design and screen printing. She has a degree in textile design and has previously worked as a freelance designer of printed textiles and wall-coverings. Her cross stitch designs have featured in many magazines including *Cross Stitch Gold*.

Acknowledgments

The publishers would like to thank the following designers for their magical contributions:
Claire Crompton, Joan Elliott, Ursula Michael, Joanne Sanderson, Lesley Teare and Carol Thornton.

Thanks to Lin Clements for managing and editing the project and preparing the charts.

Joanne Sanderson would like to thank Cara Ackerman at DMC for supplying materials.

Index